The Netherlands *p.36*
Bonn, Germany *p.128*

EUROPE

Serbia *p.162*

North Macedonia *p.18*

Marche, y *p.64*

Azerbaijan *p.162*

ASIA

Central Asian Silk Road *p.58*

Tōhoku, Japan *p.68*

Athens, Greece *p.166*

Tunisia *p.164*

Cairo, Egypt *p.118*

Dubai, UAE *p.148*

Bhutan *p.9*

Guizhou Province, China *p.82*

Madhya Pradesh, India *p.160*

NORTH PACIFIC OCEAN

Kochi, India *p.136*

AFRICA

Zanzibar, Tanzania *p.167*

East Nusa Tenggara, Indonesia *p.159*

INDIAN OCEAN

eSwatini *p.26*

AUSTRALIA

Lord Howe Island, Australia *p.78*

Cape Winelands, South Africa *p.164*

UTHERN OCEAN

BEST IN TRAVEL
2020

THE BEST IN TRAVEL PROMISE

Where is the best place to visit right now?

This is the most hotly contested topic at Lonely Planet and dominates more conversations than any other. As self-confessed travel geeks, our staff collectively rack up hundreds of thousands of miles each year, exploring almost every destination on the planet in the process.

Where is the best place to visit right now? We ask everyone at Lonely Planet, from our writers and editors all the way to our online family of social media influencers. And each year they come up with hundreds of places that are special right now, offer new things for travellers to see or do, or are criminally overlooked and underrated.

Amid fierce debate, the list is whittled down by our panel of travel experts to just 10 countries, 10 regions, 10 cities and 10 best value destinations. Each is chosen for its topicality, unique experiences and 'wow' factor. We also take sustainable travel seriously – helping you to have a positive impact wherever you choose to go.

Put simply, what remains in the pages that follow is the cream of this year's travel picks, courtesy of Lonely Planet: 10 countries, 10 regions, 10 cities, 10 best value destinations and a host of travel lists to inspire you to explore for yourself.

So what are you waiting for?

CONTENTS

LONELY PLANET'S

TOP 10
COUNTRIES

Bhutan / England / North Macedonia / Aruba / eSwatini
Costa Rica / The Netherlands / Liberia / Morocco / Uruguay

BHUTAN

A dozen nations vie for the title of real-life Shangri-La, but Bhutan's claim has more clout than most. This tiny piece of Himalayan paradise operates a strict 'high-value, low-impact' tourism policy, compelling travellers to pay a high daily fee just to set foot in its pine-scented, monastery-crowned hills. The pay-off for visitors is a chance to walk along mountain trails unsullied by litter, in the company of people whose Buddhist beliefs put them uniquely in tune with their environment. Bhutan punches well above its weight when it comes to sustainability. It is already the world's only carbon-negative country, and the kingdom is set to become the first fully organic nation by 2020, so it's only going to get more beautiful, and with the daily fee, it won't be getting any more crowded.

01

A temple in
Punakha Dzong
is decorated
with ornate
carvings

Population: 824,154
Capital: Thimphu
Language: Dzongkha
Unit of currency: Ngultrum
How to get there: Bhutan has one international airport, at Paro, served by flights from India, Nepal, Bangladesh, Thailand and Singapore. Land arrivals can enter the country from India at Phuentsholing, Gelephu and Samdrup Jongkhar.

TELL ME MORE...

If you like your mountains snow-capped, your nature untamed and your monasteries humming with the sound of Tibetan horns, look no further than Bhutan. Although entry is only possible on an organised tour, life in this intriguing backwater moves at the same tranquil pace as the prayer wheels that spin in its temple courtyards. Modern Bhutan is tucked into the bottom of mountain valleys; leave the valley floor and life slips back to an earlier time. Trekkers move in a world of rammed-earth houses, archery contests, backstrap looms, teeming wildlife – including, allegedly, the *migoi* (yeti) – and monasteries crowning each successive ridge. Informed by their Buddhist beliefs, Bhutan's people keep their mountain kingdom in pristine condition: litter is rare, pollution rarer, and the scent of blue pines wafts through the streets like incense during one of the kingdom's spectacular

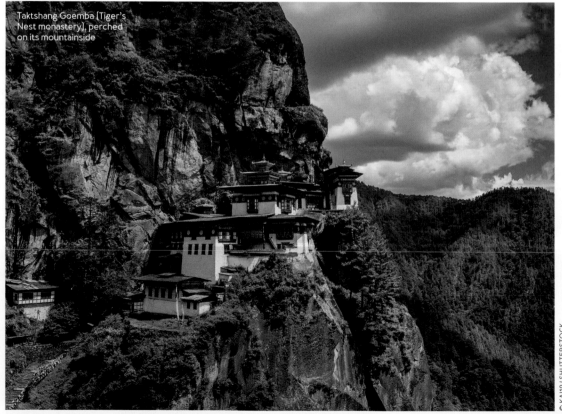

Taktshang Goemba (Tiger's Nest monastery), perched on its mountainside

© KAI19 / SHUTTERSTOCK

tsechu festivals. Breathe deeply and take in the mountain air...

UNMISSABLE EXPERIENCES
● Climb to Taktshang Goemba – it's the one must-see on almost every itinerary, yet your first glimpse of this magnificent monastery, winking through the pines from its precarious mountain vantage point, will more than justify the steep hike up here.

● Catch a *tsechu* – Bhutan's fabulous festivals bring the whole population out into the streets in traditional garb. Expect masked dances featuring fearsome deities, mystical music, clowns armed with wooden phalluses and just a little mountain magic.

● Take a spectacular trek – even in Bhutan's fast-growing capital, mountain trails are just minutes away, offering perfumed air and serene, sublime silence.

'The people of Bhutan have a great philosophy: we're the first carbon-negative country, and gross national happiness is more important to us than gross national product.'
-Ugyen Tshering, guide and driver

TIME YOUR VISIT
March to May and September to November are peak season in Bhutan, coinciding with the best weather and the clearest mountain views. Deep winter (November–March) can be bitterly cold, but there'll be fewer tourists and savings to be made; the June–August monsoon brings cloudy skies and leeches on mountain trails. October offers peak visibility; rhododendrons paint the landscape in March and April.
• By Joe Bindloss

ITINERARY
One week in Bhutan

● Start in Paro with **Paro Dzong**, a fabulous fortress that is all whitewashed walls, carved timbers and rattling prayer wheels.
● Trek to **Taktshang Goemba** (Tiger's Nest monastery), which seems to defy gravity and reality as it clings to its sheer mountain wall.
● A night in the Phobjikha valley will give you a chance to see **Gangte Goemba**, a tranquil eyrie overlooking the mountain home of black-necked cranes.
● Next visit **Punakha Dzong**, famed as Bhutan's most beautiful fortress, framed by jacaranda trees at the confluence of two sacred rivers.
● Photographers will love the **National Institute for Zorig Chusum**, an esteemed Thimphu college where gifted Bhutanese youngsters train in the country's 13 traditional arts.

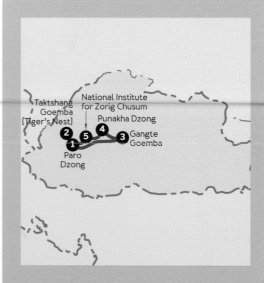

Dancers in masks
and traditional dress
perform in a *tsechu*

Durdle Door, a rock formation on England's Jurassic Coast

02

ENGLAND

Once the country's first line of defence against invaders, the English coastline these days is a peaceful place where locals and visitors can enjoy more tranquil pursuits. Taking a bracing walk on a windswept pier, eating delicious fish and chips, searching for marine life in rockpools, finding fossils in ancient cliffs, building sandcastles and dolphin-spotting on picturesque beaches are just some of the activities offered by the English seaside. And indulging in these and more activities is set to become a whole lot easier with the 2020 launch of the England Coast Path, the longest continuous trail of its kind in the world, which promises access to the country's entire coastline for the first time.

Population: 55.6 million
Capital: London
Language: English
Unit of currency: Pound sterling
How to get there: London's five airports have flights to virtually everywhere on the planet. Outside the capital, Manchester in the north has worldwide connections, and the country's many smaller local airports have flights to Europe and beyond.

TELL ME MORE...

Brexit uncertainties have dominated the headlines in recent years but one constant amid all the confusion has been the timeless treasures that England is famous for. The historic castles and cathedrals, the quaint villages and

'The English coast in all its glory – plunging cliffs, golden curls of sand, flapping sailboats fighting the wind, endless "What's out there?" sea views – is also where the country's quirks tend to wash up, like the gold buried in Folkestone.'
-Daniel Fahey, writer and Folkestone resident

rolling countryside and, of course, the seaside. Nowhere in England is more than 110km from the coast, and the English love of beach holidays is a longstanding tradition. Access, though, has sometimes been an issue, with sections of the shore cut off from the public, but a huge campaign by the Ramblers, a group dedicated to making England accessible to all, successfully persuaded the government back in 2014 to commit to a full England Coast Path by 2020. Although many sections already existed, it's been no easy task joining the dots to create the 4800km trail. But determination has paid off

ITINERARY
Two weeks in England

● Famed for hills, lakes and literary connections, the **Lake District** is also the start of the Coast to Coast Walk.
● Gentle valleys with cute villages make the **Yorkshire Dales** a joy. Grab some celebrated Wensleydale cheese.
● With an unrivalled history, **York** is the place to delve into England's past – and try a Yorkshire rascal (cake) at the famous Bettys cafe.
● The **North York Moors'** bleak beauty is best enjoyed on a steam-train ride – then keep walking to Robin Hood's Bay: the end of the Coast to Coast Walk.
● After all that walking, head to **Bath** and rest your limbs in the spa waters like the Romans did. The shopping and Georgian architecture here are superlative.
● Finish with a night in the capital, **London**. Dine out in Soho, then head to a show in Theatreland.

and now anyone who wants to walk from Berwick-upon-Tweed in the country's northeast to Bowness-on-Solway in the northwest just needs a sturdy pair of boots (and a detour via the Wales Coast Path, the world's first national coast path when it opened in 2012).

UNMISSABLE EXPERIENCES

● Northumberland's coast is a magical history tour, home to dramatic castles, offshore islands with puffins and seals, and the spectacular Holy Island, accessible only at low tide across a causeway.

● Walk, cycle, or jump on the Coasthopper bus: however you see it, the Norfolk Coast, a designated Area of Outstanding Natural Beauty for over 50 years, is one of England's most attractive sections of coastline.

● A pioneer of seaside access, the South West Coast Path takes the long way round from Somerset to Dorset. Originally developed to patrol for smugglers, these days it's hikers who come for its wonderful walks and photogenic views.

TIME YOUR VISIT

There's no guarantee of good weather at any time during the English year. More important for tackling the coast is coming prepared – good walking shoes and waterproofs are essential. Summer crowds on some sections can be off-putting, and you're just as likely to see the sun in the quieter spring and autumn. To enjoy the trails with like-minded visitors, join a walking group – there are dozens across the country.

• By Clifton Wilkinson

A wreath of mist covers the valley below Hadrian's Wall, Northumberland

© JUSTIN FOULKES / LONELY PLANET

Bath Abbey is reflected in the still waters of the Roman Baths

© JUSTIN BLACK / SHUTTERSTOCK

NORTH MACEDONIA

███ **'Best of' travel lists brim** with anniversaries and airport openings. Rare is the opportunity to celebrate the rebranding of a country. Such is the case for North Macedonia – a place most know simply as Macedonia – which claimed a fresh moniker after decades of political debate with bordering Greece. The agreement, signed in 2018, provided a feel-good moment of neighbourly love and a revamped international image for the tiny nation in the heart of the Balkans. It's already renowned for gastronomy, ancient tradition and nature, but culture junkies and adventurers will find new excuses to visit in 2020 with the addition of flight routes to Unesco-protected Lake Ohrid and the recently launched High Scardus Trail, a 495km trek along the region's most dramatic peaks.

© DANKEI / SHUTTERSTOCK

The Church of Sveti Jovan overlooks Lake Ohrid

03

'To get away, I hike in the Shar Mountains, where the food, wine and adventures are real. The term "authentic" is used too easily, but that really defines North Macedonia.'
-Aleksandar Donev, director of eco-adventure tour operator Mustseedonia

Population: 2.1 million
Capital: Skopje
Languages: Macedonian, Albanian
Unit of currency: Macedonian denar
How to get there: For most visitors, Skopje International Airport, 21km from the capital and North Macedonia's main airport, is the logical option for arriving in this landlocked country. There is, with the addition of new Wizz Air routes, also a growing list of European flights servicing St Paul the Apostle Airport in Ohrid, a tourism hub. Overland, there are regular international bus and train options (especially to Skopje), with buses being the more modern, reliable and popular choice.

Traditional Macedonian folk costumes

TELL ME MORE...
More than just a novel passport stamp, the country's new title spotlights southeast Europe's very foundations. North Macedonia has been the intersection between civilisations since before recorded history. Greek, Macedonian, Roman, Byzantine and Ottoman traditions dovetailed here to create the type of destination today's travellers demand: old-world experiences, architecture from every epoch, untouched wilderness, an ancient wine reputation and day-long meals with local ingredients over which to recount all the adventures. In capital Skopje, bisected by the Vardar River and lined with cafes, a hilltop fortress and bazaar provide the backdrop for museums and bistros. Further south, Lake Ohrid – now serviced by a slew of Wizz Air flights – is one of the continent's oldest and deepest lakes (more than one million years old and some 300m deep). And stitching the country together, long-distance hiking trails, such as the new High Scardus Trail and the trans-Balkan Via Dinarica trekking route, traverse mountain ranges straddling the borders with Kosovo and Albania.

UNMISSABLE EXPERIENCES
● Skopje's Ottoman Bazaar, or Čaršija, has been a buzzing market for more than five centuries. Today, the flagstone pedestrian-only avenues are a stroll through time filled with craftspeople and cafes.
● A hike to the 2498m Mt Ljuboten, the Shar mountain range's northernmost peak, supplies

© IOAN FLORIN CNEJEVICI | GETTY IMAGES

ITINERARY
Ten days in North Macedonia

● Combine eras in **Skopje** by visiting the 6th-century Tvrdina Kale Fortress, Ottoman Bazaar, Museum of Contemporary Art and trendy Debar Maalo neighbourhood.

● Saddle up in the mountainside village of **Galičnik** for a horseback tour of Mavrovo National Park.

● Tour the **Ohrid** region, Unesco-inscribed since 1979, and its ancient, fresco-covered, lakeside monasteries and churches.

● Boat to the island of **Golem Grad** in Lake Prespa to see Roman ruins. Then lounge on sandy **Dupeni Beach** on the lake's eastern shore.

● In the country's centre, taste the reds, whites and rosés in the **Tikveš Wine District** – among the country's, and Balkans', most famous.

epic ridgeline views along Kosovo's border. After the climb, overnight in Villa Ljuboten, where grilled meats, fresh peppers, and *rakija* (local schnapps) await.

● In mid-July, Galičnik, a village on the slopes of Bistra Mountain, hosts a wedding festival. The two-day affair, attended by thousands of locals and travellers, overflows with traditional food, music, toasts and true love.

TIME YOUR VISIT
June to August is North Macedonia's high season. However, savvy travellers will avoid the crowds by visiting in the shoulder seasons of late spring (especially for Skopje) and early autumn (for superb hiking). In the winter, the ski resorts at Mavrovo and Popova Šapka offer solid conditions for every ability.

• By Alex Crevar

ARUBA

In Aruba's south, the cultural hub of San Nicolas, known as Sunrise City, is relishing a colourful and creative revival, with international and local artists adorning street walls and pop-up carnival experiences extending the happy vibes beyond the annual festivities. Equally important and worth celebrating is the country's planned transition to 100% renewable energy in 2020, alongside a total ban on single-use plastics (bring a bottle, the tap water is drinkable) and reef-destroying sunscreens. With a flurry of new home-sharing accommodation and experiences on offer, an authentic, more affordable, and sustainable Aruba awaits among its palm-fringed and pristine beaches.

Aruba's divi divi trees are bent by the trade winds

© STEVE PHOTOGRAPHY | SHUTTERSTOCK

Population: 106,000

Capital: Oranjestad

Languages: Papiamento, Dutch (official); Spanish, English (commonly spoken)

Unit of currency: Aruban florin, with US dollars also accepted in most establishments

How to get there: Reina Beatrix International Airport offers regular flight routes to North and South America. Daily flights from Amsterdam and weekly flights from the UK provide connections in Europe. Cruise ships arrive into the capital, Oranjestad.

'I love the friendly people, beautiful nature and year-round perfect weather, but my favourite thing to do in Aruba is to rent a jeep and discover the national park and north coast with its remote beaches and one-of-a-kind landscape.'

-David Troeger, photographer at Jetlag Creative Studio

TELL ME MORE...

Bon bini, Papiamento for 'welcome', is a phrase you'll not just hear regularly in Aruba, but genuinely feel, in no small part thanks to the infectious smiles of the locals.

The island's famed white sands and lapping waves offer plenty of beachside relaxation, while water-sports fanatics can indulge in a plethora of options, from stand-up paddleboarding on calm waters to kitesurfing the windswept coast. Multiple shipwrecks make Aruba a prime scuba-diving destination, and with a ban on sunscreens containing oxybenzone being introduced in 2020, protection of the reefs is paramount.

Inland, the landscape provides a stark contrast, from the arid Arikok National Park,

ITINERARY
One week in Aruba

● Discover the island's culture in the capital city, **Oranjestad**, sprinkled with splashy colonial buildings. Aruba Walking Tours provides an easy-to-digest history tour with stops to sample the island's multicultural food offerings.

● Hit the waters in the rugged north, where you can kayak or stand-up paddleboard against the impressive **California Lighthouse** backdrop, before enjoying the sunset and some enchanting stargazing among the desolate **California Dunes**.

● Adventure through **Arikok National Park**, from its arid and aloe-carpeted glory to the jagged, cerulean-hued coastline.

● Sample the artistic soul of Aruba in **San Nicolas**, where the streets are adorned with vibrant murals, and the Cosecha Creative Center provides workshops and goods from local artists.

Dutch colonial buildings
overlook Oranjestad's
harbour

an ecotourism destination partly reserved for research, to the wetlands of the Bubali Bird Sanctuary. Hiking and bike trails provide a sustainable alternative to exploring by 4WD, while wellness activities such as t'ai chi and yoga are readily available, meaning a visit to Aruba is good for both your soul and Mother Nature.

UNMISSABLE EXPERIENCES

● Celebrate the kaleidoscopic spirit of the island during the Aruba Carnival, the nation's joyful jamboree held annually between January and February. A new museum dedicated to the history of Carnival is also opening in San Nicolas.

● Hike or bike through the craggy and cactus-consumed scenery of Arikok National Park to the wave-smashed east coast. Take a dip in one of the natural swimming pools and explore cave paintings from the island's earliest inhabitants, the Caquetio.

● Picturesque beaches are synonymous with Aruba, but below the crystal-clear waters, scuba divers can venture to the USS *Antilla* shipwreck, and savour the unique opportunity of diving two sunken aircraft, now transitioning into blossoming artificial reefs.

TIME YOUR VISIT

Aruba sits below the hurricane belt, though heavier rainfall and some storms are usual between September and December. January and February see the streets come alive with costumes and parades for Carnival, while Aruba Art Fair occurs in September. Although it's busy year-round, April to September tends to offer lower prices on accommodation.

• By Daniel James Clarke

TOP 10 COUNTRIES

ESWATINI

▬▬▬ **Petite, pleasant and packed with** culture, adventure and legendary wildlife, the newly named Kingdom of eSwatini (formerly Swaziland) is one of Southern Africa's most underrated (and least visited) destinations. A new international airport, as well as improved road infrastructure between it, conservation areas and the capital, are aimed to increase visitor numbers in the years ahead – get here in 2020 to ensure yourself a front seat. The varied landscapes within its parks and reserves provide one exciting revelation after another, whether it's zip lining, trekking, whitewater rafting or mind-blowing rhino encounters. Mix in a pervading sense of peace and enthralling cultural festivities and you'll be smiling all the way home.

Zebras run wild in Mlilwane Wildlife Sanctuary

© MAX_ON_AIR / GETTY IMAGES

05

Population: 1.1 million
Capital: Mbabane
Languages: Swati, English
Unit of currency: Swazi lilangeni
(plural emalangeni)
How to get there: There are
daily flights into King Mswati
III International Airport from
Johannesburg, but most people
enter overland by rental car
through one of the many border
crossings with South Africa.

TELL ME MORE...

The land of King Mswati III, eSwatini
is Africa's last absolute monarchy.
As such, there are many traditions
that still continue here as they have
done in centuries past. No two are
greater than the sacred Incwala
ceremony and the Umhlanga (reed)
Dance Festival – both provide an
incredible chance to witness and
pay respect to Swazi culture. Other
traditions are less obvious, but they
underline the palpable warmth and
enduring nature of your day-to-day
interactions with Swazis during your
travels. This is a laid-back nation that
lacks the urban tensions often felt in

'eSwatini is a people place.
So much so that it doesn't
feel right to walk past
someone, anyone, without
greeting them. In fact, our
local "hello" is "sawubona",
which means "I see you".'
-Darron Raw, managing director of
Swazi Trails

A lion suns himself in Hlane
Royal National Park

© PAL TERAVAGIMOV PHOTOGRAPHY / GETTY IMAGES

Women in traditional
costumes march at the
Umhlanga Dance Festival

© HOMO COSMICOS / SHUTTERSTOCK

ITINERARY
A week in eSwatini

● Allow at least a day to explore the country's largest protected area, **Hlane Royal National Park,** while on safari for lions, leopards, rhinos and elephants.

● Continue your wildlife extravaganza in **Mkhaya Game Reserve,** which offers unparalleled rhino experiences.

● Battle white water on a full- or half-day rafting trip on the **Great Usutu River.**

● Peruse the market in **Manzini** or those in the Malkerns Valley for Swazi craft treasures.

● Finish with a chilled horseback or mountain bike safari experience in **Mlilwane Wildlife Sanctuary,** and/or amp up the adventure with a hike and zip-line tour in the mountains of **Malolotja Nature Reserve.**

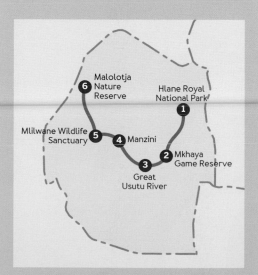

neighbouring South Africa. Sustained conservation efforts have ensured your encounters with eSwatini's wildlife are also unforgettable, with Mkhaya Game Reserve providing perhaps the best rhino encounters on the entire continent – some of these even take place with you on foot. Mlilwane Wildlife Sanctuary is another standout, where you can actually mingle among herds of wildebeests and zebras while on horseback.

UNMISSABLE EXPERIENCES

● Standing in stunned silence while watching a crash of almost a dozen wild rhinos bathe, lounge and drink at one of the many secluded waterholes within Mkhaya Game Reserve, a refuge for both the black and white species.

● Spotting zebras, elands, wildebeests, warthogs and more while on a short stroll, day hike or challenging multi-day trek in the rough mountain terrain of Malolotja Nature Reserve (the 10-stage zip-line canopy tour here is also a must).

● Being a respectful observer of one of the continent's greatest cultural events, the Umhlanga Dance Festival, which is held at the usually off-limits Eludzidzini Royal Residence near Lobamba.

TIME YOUR VISIT

The main parks are rewarding year-round. However, with fewer water sources causing wildlife to congregate, and thinner foliage increasing sight lines in the bush, the dry season (May to September) is best for safaris. The Umhlanga Dance Festival takes place during the first week of September, with the main event happening on the 7th.

• By Matt Phillips

06

COSTA RICA

Costa Rica flies the flag for sustainable tourism. This small country's vast biodiversity attracts visitors keen to spot sleepy sloths in trees, red-eyed frogs paralysing their predators, and whales in the Pacific. Costa Ricans understand the importance of preserving their slice of tropical paradise and have found a way to invite others in while living in harmony with their neighbours – from leafcutter ants to jaguars. Ninety per cent of the country's energy is created by renewable sources, and it could become one of the first carbon-neutral countries in 2020. Adventure lovers can hike volcanoes or ride a zip line, while those craving 'me time' can enjoy yoga retreats and spa experiences. The catchphrase *pura vida* (pure life) is more than a saying, it's a way of life.

Trekking through the dense jungle near Quepos

© KATHRIN ZIEGLER / GETTY IMAGES

31

Population: 5 million
Capital: San José
Language: Spanish
Unit of currency: Costa Rican colón
How to get there: Costa Rica has two international airports. The majority of flights arrive into Juan Santamaría, 20km west of San José. There's also an airport close to Liberia in the north of the country, which is a great option for exploring the Pacific Coast. Alternatively, you can enter Costa Rica overland via one of its neighbours, Nicaragua and Panama.

TELL ME MORE...

With 25% of its land protected, Costa Rica is a place to embrace the great outdoors. And how biodiverse is this eco-paradise? Covering just 0.03% of the world's surface area, it's home to 5% of the planet's species. In reality, you're unlikely to go more than a day before encountering a lizard, a monkey or a snake! Between wildlife encounters, expect to feast on simple meals of grilled chicken or fish with a side of *gallo pinto*, a flavoursome dish of rice and beans. Add a dollop of Salsa Lizano, a spiced condiment found on every table, and you'll soon be living like a Costa Rican. Fuelled up and ready for another adventure, catch some world-class surf at Playa Tamarindo or navigate the ferocious rapids rafting down the Pacuare River.

'My favourite place in Costa Rica is Monteverde. I love watching the moisture-filled clouds drifting across the forest, enriching the ecosystem. We are one of the happiest societies on the planet, and I love seeing tourists enjoying our unique country.'
-Carlos Vargas, owner of Vargas Tours

ITINERARY
Two weeks in Costa Rica

● Relax with visits to hot springs and waterfalls close to **La Fortuna**, with the looming 1670m peak of Volcán Arenal as its backdrop.

● Delve into lush cloud forests, scream your way along Central America's longest zip line, or sip some of the country's finest coffee in **Monteverde**.

● Take a walk on the wild side in **Corcovado National Park**, spotting sloths, monkeys, snakes, toucans, frogs and whales in their natural habitats.

● Rent a kayak in **Tortuguero National Park** for more animal encounters, before learning about the leatherback, hawksbill and green sea turtles that call the beaches home.

● Finish your trip enjoying the Rasta vibes in **Puerto Viejo de Talamanca**.

An iguana clings to a cactus
in Corcovado National Park

UNMISSABLE EXPERIENCES

● Wake to the sound of howler monkeys and spend a day exploring Corcovado or Manuel Antonio National Park. Watch halloween crabs scuttling along pristine beaches, coatimundis clambering up palm trees, and hear the squawks of scarlet macaws flying overhead.

● From the Pacific Coast head out on a boat to see humpback whales enjoying warmer waters on their annual winter vacation.

● Spend a memorable night listening to sounds of the rainforest at Lapa Rios, one of Costa Rica's unique ecolodges. With nets for windows, and a wild rainforest outside that's home to monkeys, toucans, frogs, macaws and more, you'll have never felt closer to nature.

TIME YOUR VISIT

With two coasts and several microclimates, weather across the country is extremely varied. The Pacific Coast is driest December to April, while the Caribbean's dry season falls between March and September. Your greatest chance to see humpback whales is from August to October. Regardless of when you visit, it's a tropical country so be prepared for rain; you'll be rewarded with lush rainforests.

• By Chloe Gunning

Catarata Río Fortuna
(La Fortuna Waterfall)
thunders down a canyon in
Volcán Arenal National Park

THE NETHERLANDS

In the year that marks 75 years of freedom since the end of WWII, the Netherlands is ready to celebrate with events across the country. Vibrant Amsterdam is always ready to party, but by making use of the excellent train network you can explore a host of celebrations in stunning cities and get more bang for your euros. April and May are the months to visit, as you can take in Kingsday, Liberation Day and the Eurovision Song Contest, which will be hosted in the country this year. Set out on the ever-growing network of over 35,000km of cycling paths to explore attractions beyond the cities, such as Unesco World Heritage Site the Wadden Sea, and discover the wealth of nature that this tiny country has to offer.

Historic ships line the Hoge der A canal of Groningen

07

© CLA78 / SHUTTERSTOCK

Cube Houses
(Kubuswoningen) by
architect Piet Blom, in
Rotterdam

Population: 17 million
Capital: Amsterdam
Languages: Dutch
Unit of currency: Euro

How to get there: Schiphol Airport is the biggest airport in the Netherlands, but there are smaller ones in Groningen, Rotterdam, Eindhoven and Maastricht. In addition, the Netherlands is easily reached by train from many European destinations, now including the UK, thanks to the new direct Eurostar line connecting Amsterdam and London.

TELL ME MORE...

A visit to the Netherlands isn't complete without a stop in Amsterdam. Taking a stroll alongside the canal houses is more serene than ever, as boating heads to an all-electric future. The crowds remain ever-present, though – hop aboard a train to leave them behind and visit less-explored cities such as Groningen, Maastricht or Eindhoven. Join the friendly locals for a cold beer in a pub and visit top-notch restaurants (increasingly catering to vegetarians and vegans), craft breweries, and museums filled with masterpieces. Wherever you decide to go, it's never hard to take a break from city life. Explore the Unesco-listed Wadden Sea, spot highland cows on a hike across the Veluwe or take a sailing trip on one of the many Frisian lakes. The best way to discover it all? By doing as the locals do and jumping on a bike of course.

UNMISSABLE EXPERIENCES

● In the 'Green Heart' (the natural area surrounded by Den Haag, Rotterdam, Utrecht and Amsterdam), adventure company Hihahut provides four unique cabins connected by hiking, bike and boating routes. Create your own Hihahut-adventure by linking visits to these sustainable places to stay; you could sleep in a tent in a greenhouse or a cabin in an orchard with a see-through roof made for stargazing.
● The Wadden Sea boasts five Dutch islands all worth a visit. For the full experience, embark on a guided 'mud walk' across the bottom of

The Kinderdijk Cycle Route passes historic windmills

© COMANICIU DAN / SHUTTERSTOCK

'Living here means being and believing what you want. The Dutch are open-minded and multilingual, making it easy to feel at home. In my home town, Groningen, visit Pernikkel for a late breakfast!'

-Fareeda van der Marel, head chef at restaurant Achterwerk

the sea at low tide and experience the power of its ebb and flow while hiking to Ameland or Schiermonnikoog from the mainland.

TIME YOUR VISIT

April 2020 has been declared the Month of Freedom, with the national Liberation Day on 5 May as a cumulative highlight. On this day, fourteen Freedom Festivals will be held throughout the country. Visiting in April brings the added bonus of being able to celebrate Kingsday with the locals on the 27th.

• By Linda Ismaili

ITINERARY
One week in the Netherlands

● Starting off in **Amsterdam**, hop aboard a ferry to the lesser-known north of the city. Spend the day hunting for vintage treasures, and then find a spot by the riverside at Pllek to sample some local beers. Then leave the crowds behind and explore the country by train – the furthest stop is less than 2½ hours away.

● Take a walking tour in **Rotterdam** to discover its innovative architecture and harrowing war history.

● Take a day-trip from historical **Arnhem** and cycle across **Hoge Veluwe National Park** to admire Van Goghs at the Kröller-Müller Museum.

● Explore **Groningen**'s cosy and car-free city centre, where bars don't have a closing time and the countryside is just a bike ride away.

Groningen 5

Amsterdam 1

Hoge Veluwe
National Park 4

Arnhem 3

Rotterdam 2

Last daylight falls on a field of tulips near Zijldijk, Groningen

08

TOP 10 COUNTRIES

LIBERIA

▬▬▬▬ **For most outsiders,** Liberia is a bit of a mystery. But those in the know wax lyrical about the optimism of its people and the country's natural wonders. There are idyllic beaches, washed by some of West Africa's best surf at low-key resorts such as Robertsport. Then there's Sapo National Park, the second-largest area of primary rainforest in West Africa. In these dense forests, you stand a chance of running into chimpanzees, forest elephants and Liberia's famous pygmy hippos – no larger than a Shetland pony. Better still, a groundbreaking development deal with Norway to halt all deforestation by 2020 looks set to keep this natural treasure safe for generations.

Sunset over
Liberia's
protected
rainforest

'When travelling in Liberia, you can feel the untapped potential of its natural beauty. Liberia is blessed with lush rainforests, rivers, lakes and miles of unspoiled beaches, all ready to be discovered.'

-Geert Van Dorst, Paynesville resident and founder of VisitLiberia.net

Liberia's forests and swamps are home to the pygmy hippopotamus

© VLADIMIR WRANGEL / SHUTTERSTOCK

Population: 4.7 million

Capital: Monrovia

Languages: English

Unit of currency: Liberian dollar

How to get there: Most visitors to Liberia arrive by air; flights into Monrovia Roberts International Airport from outside Africa generally involve a stop in Nairobi or another African hub. Adventurous travellers can enter overland, using a mixture of buses and bush-taxis, from Côte d'Ivoire, Guinea and Sierra Leone.

TELL ME MORE...

Founded as a homeland for freed American slaves, but often confused with the similar state for British freedmen in Sierra Leone, Liberia is one of Africa's smallest and least known republics. Just a few years ago the country was making headlines for all the wrong reasons, but in 2016 it was given a clean bill of health, and today this small, surprising nation has riches that belie its troubled past: Sapo National Park, with chimps and pygmy hippos wandering through 1808 sq km of virgin rainforest; gold-spun beaches and barrelling surf at Robertsport; forest elephants crashing through the undergrowth in newly protected Gola Forest National Park. Superimposed over this African tableau is a hint of the American south: Liberia's fading antebellum architecture pays homage to the great plantation houses of Mississippi and Louisiana. Angling for a brighter future, an aid-for-conservation deal with Norway could be a turning point in preserving one of the largest surviving areas of rainforest in Africa; visit now, and you may have Liberia's beaches, breaks and brilliant green almost to yourself.

UNMISSABLE EXPERIENCES

● Sapo National Park preserves 40% of the Upper Guinean rainforest, providing refuge for a string of signature species. Taking a safari here feels like proper exploration, rather than the tamed-down-for-tourists version.

A peaceful moment on one of Monrovia's beautiful beaches

© EDWIN REMSBERG / ALAMY STOCK PHOTO

ITINERARY
One week in Liberia

● Explore abandoned architecture in **Monrovia** – on top of beaches and museums, the capital is dotted with once-grand buildings left in ruins by the civil war.

● Visit **Robertsport** for some tube-riding: Cotton Trees and Cassava Point are the best-loved breaks at Liberia's favourite surf strip.

● Go beach-hopping around **Buchanan**, using this port city as a base for wild camping trips along the coast, far from even Liberia's modest crowds.

● Head for **Sapo National Park** to see chimps, elephants, leopards and pygmy hippos roaming in this vast sprawl of virgin forest.

● Stop in **Harper** to visit William Tubman Mansion, the former home of a president, among other atmospheric ruins scattered around this fascinating backwater.

● Catch a wave in Robertsport. Breaks barrel with satisfying consistency from March to October in this laid-back surf centre, whose buzz is growing.

● Being the only tourist in town is a common experience in many parts of the country; only adventurers roam far beyond the capital and Robertsport.

TIME YOUR VISIT

The dry months from December to July are the best time to travel on Liberia's mainly unsurfaced roads; prices peak in December and January coinciding with the main tourist season. Conversely, the rainy months from May to October bring the best swells to Liberia's surf beaches, but also tropical storms.

• By Joe Bindloss

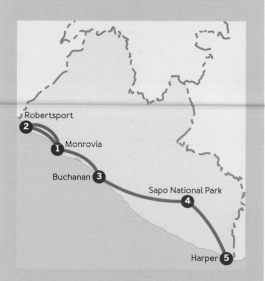

Robertsport ②

Monrovia ①

Buchanan ③

Sapo National Park ④

Harper ⑤

09
BEST IN
TRAVEL
2020

MOROCCO

Morocco is having a moment, with time-honoured attractions complemented by sustainable-yet-stylish lodging, restaurants serving up seasonal produce and coastal wellness retreats mixing up yoga and surfing. And thanks to improved infrastructure it's easier to get around by road, while Africa's first high-speed train means that you can zip from Casablanca to Tangier in just two hours. Ancient medinas are getting a makeover in Fez, Essaouira, Meknes, Tetouan and Marrakesh, which will be crowned Africa's first Capital of Culture in 2020 in celebration of its rich heritage. And you can still escape the crowds in Berber mountain villages, deserted Atlantic beaches and far-flung desert outposts.

Marrakesh's Djemaa El Fna comes alive in the early evening

09

Traditional doorway of the Medersa Bou Inania in Fez

'Morocco's rich and diverse culture combined with intricate layers of society offers a unique perspective on ancient traditions juxtaposed with a contemporary, constantly evolving society.'

-Michele Reeves, owner/director of Plan-it Morocco

Population: 35.7 million

Capital: Rabat

Languages: Arabic (official language), Tamazight (official Amazigh/Berber language), French

Unit of currency: Moroccan dirham

How to get there: The easiest way is to fly, with wallet-friendly direct flights from Europe to Marrakesh, Fez, Casablanca, Tangier, Rabat, Agadir and Essaouira, with Casablanca the main entry point for flights from the US, Australia, Asia and the Middle East. From Spain, the fast ferry takes an hour from Tarifa to Tangier City Port and 1½ hours from Algeciras to Tangier Med, 40km away.

TELL ME MORE...

If variety is the spice of life, Morocco has it in spades. One day you could be scaling Toubkal, North Africa's highest peak, the next you could be surfing in Taghazout, strolling through the twisting blue alleyways of Chefchaouen or cycling through Marrakesh on a tour that supports young Moroccans. Culture vultures can dip into world-class museums – perhaps the Yves Saint Laurent Museum or the Women's Museum (a North African first) in Marrakesh – take a literary tour in Tangier or lose themselves in the world's largest living medieval medina in Fez. Art lovers will enjoy the galleries of Gueliz, the street art of Asilah and the self-taught artists of Essaouira, while in Casablanca architecture buffs will find everything from art deco to brutalism, alongside one of Africa's largest mosques showcasing Morocco's finest decorative arts. There's fun for foodies with

ITINERARY
Two weeks in Morocco

● Explore the medina, monuments and museums of **Marrakesh**, starting with Africa's most famous square, the Djemaa El Fna.

● Hike among the rolling hills, secret valleys and earthen villages of the **High Atlas Mountains** with a local guide, sleeping in a kasbah-turned-lodge staffed by villagers.

● Head to the desert, stopping off at the *ksar* (fortified village) of **Aït Ben Haddou**, with verdant palm oases and dramatic gorges en route.

● Marvel at the dunes of **Erg Chebbi** before drinking mint tea in the Sahara under a blanket of stars at an eco-friendly tented camp.

● Relax in the laid-back coastal city of **Essaouira** with its *Game of Thrones* fortress, blue fishing boats bobbing in the harbour and perfect kitesurfing conditions.

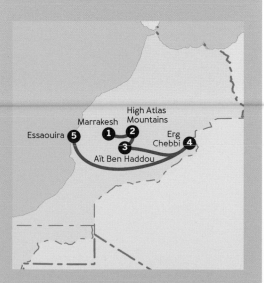

cooking classes, street food tours and homegrown chefs creating a gourmet take on traditional dishes. And accommodation is equally diverse, from surfer-chic hostels to palatial riads, contemporary boutiques to rustic desert camps.

UNMISSABLE EXPERIENCES

● The imperial cities of Fez and Marrakesh were both capitals during Morocco's long and fascinating history and are famed for their mesmerising medinas, vibrant souqs and extravagant monuments.

● There's a festival for all musical tastes: the Fes Festival of World Sacred Music, Casablanca's Jazzablanca, the global stars of Rabat's Mawazine, Essaouira's Gnaoua World Music Festival and Timitar Festival's celebration of Amazigh music in Agadir.

● Morocco's a shopper's paradise, with labyrinthine souqs where copper beaters and leather workers still ply their trades. A new wave of concept stores sees Moroccan designers working with local artisans to give age-old crafts a contemporary twist.

TIME YOUR VISIT

Spring (March–June) and autumn (September–November), when the weather is warm and dry, are the best times to explore inland cities and the southern desert. Head to the High Atlas Mountains from June to September. When temperatures soar in the height of summer, head to the coast. If you visit during Ramadan, the month of fasting (estimated dates for 2020 are 24 April to 23 May), be discreet about eating and drinking during the day.

• By Sarah Gilbert

A camel caravan makes its way through the sand dunes of Erg Chigaga

URUGUAY

If Uruguay isn't already on your South American bucket list, 2020 is the perfect year to add it. While economic and political turmoil roil much of the continent, Uruguay stands as an oasis of calm stability: an advanced, developed nation that has proudly championed a progressive social agenda in recent years – from marijuana legalisation to the open embrace of LGBTQ+ rights. Uruguay regularly wins plaudits as South America's only 'full democracy' and a leader in sustainable tourism and eco-friendliness. But what visitors remember most are Uruguay's laid-back, welcoming and down-to-earth people and the subtle but profound beauty of the country's landscape – from the long, untamed Atlantic coastline to the boundless open spaces of the pampas.

The esplanade of Piriápolis, on Rocha's coast

© ELOJOTORPE / GETTY IMAGES

'The cliff of La Pedrera is like a balcony into the sea. From there you can see whales, big waves, surfers and paragliders. The grandeur of the ocean is breathtaking.'
-Mónica Pérez Peñaflor, artist & co-owner,
El Galope Hostel & Horse Farm

Population: 3.4 million
Capital: Montevideo
Language: Spanish
Unit of currency: Uruguayan peso
How to get there: Direct flights serve Montevideo's Carrasco International Airport from Buenos Aires, São Paulo, Santiago, Miami and Madrid. Frequent ferries cross from Argentina to Colonia del Sacramento, Carmelo and Montevideo.

TELL ME MORE…

With 660km of Río de la Plata and Atlantic shoreline, a burgeoning wine industry, bubbling hot springs and endless rolling rangelands where South America's grandeur feels seductively tangible, Uruguay has something for everyone. Hub city Montevideo is one of South America's most cosmopolitan capitals, with a thriving cultural scene that runs the gamut from nightly *milongas* (tango gatherings) to colourful multi-week Carnaval celebrations. West and east, respectively, the tourist magnets of Colonia del Sacramento and Punta del Este offer cobblestoned colonial charm and glitzy flash-your-suntan glamour. Further afield, authentic ecotourism experiences derived from longstanding local ties to the land are everywhere – choose from horseback rides under Uruguay's wide-open skies, birdwatching floats on coastal lagoons fringed by ancient *ombú*

La Mano (The Hand) is a sculpture located at Brava Beach in Punta del Este

trees, or cetacean-spotting in the proposed South Atlantic Whale Sanctuary. Throughout the country, Uruguay's modern, inexpensive buses make travelling a breeze, whisking you wherever you like within a half day or less.

UNMISSABLE EXPERIENCES

● Wander tree-shaded 17th-century streets and plazas and enjoy stunning Río de la Plata sunsets in Colonia del Sacramento, a historic river port long contested by the Portuguese and Spanish, now a favourite weekend getaway for visiting Argentines.

● Brave the bumpy ride over the sand dunes to Cabo Polonio – an isolated fishing community on a long, lonely Atlantic beach thronged with sea lions and crowned by a picturesque lighthouse.

© ELBUD / SHUTTERSTOCK

ITINERARY
Two weeks in Uruguay

● Ferry through the island-dotted Paraná Delta to **Carmelo**, where you can cycle and wine-taste your way through award-winning Tannat vineyards.

● Hit **Montevideo**'s museums and beaches by day, then linger into late evening at the capital's countless bars, restaurants and clubs.

● Cruise up Rocha's wild lagoon-dotted coast, pausing to surf at **La Pedrera** or canter down the beach at **Punta del Diablo**.

● Follow galloping gauchos and scurrying rheas into Uruguay's big-skied interior, overnighting at an *estancia* near **Tacuarembó** or in the idyllic Valle del Lunarejo.

● Stop for a soak at Termas San Nicanor, one of several hot springs near **Salto** on the Río Uruguay.

● Experience life on a working *estancia* (ranch), helping herd cattle on horseback, enjoying traditional Uruguayan *asados* (barbecues), and sharing *yerba mate* tea and fireside conversation late into the night.

TIME YOUR VISIT
Crowds convene and prices skyrocket from Christmas to the end of January at such coastal hotspots as Punta del Este. For fine beach weather without the midsummer crush, visit in February or March, when you can also catch street theatre during Montevideo's Carnaval and celebrate gaucho culture at Tacuarembó's gaucho festival. To see whales frolicking off the Atlantic coast, come between July and October.
• By Gregor Clark

LONELY PLANET'S

TOP 10
REGIONS

Central Asian Silk Road / Le Marche, Italy / Tōhoku, Japan

Maine, USA / Lord Howe Island, Australia / Guizhou Province, China

Cadiz Province, Spain / Northeast Argentina

Kvarner Gulf, Croatia / Brazilian Amazon

TOP 10 REGIONS

CENTRAL ASIAN SILK ROAD

▬▬▬▬ **A region once made rich** by trade and travellers, the Central Asian Silk Road is again at the centre of global interest. The ancient cities, bustling bazaars and wild landscapes of Central Asia are drawing increasing numbers of visitors looking for adventure along one of history's most storied travel routes. Kyrgyzstan, Tajikistan and Uzbekistan all now offer either visa-free access or e-visas for the majority of the world's citizens; and the region is moving towards a unified 'Silk Road' visa. Meanwhile massive transportation and infrastructure investment – much of it under the aegis of China's Belt and Road Initiative – make travelling the modern Silk Road more accessible than ever before.

01

Uzbekistan's
Registan is
a stunning
ensemble of
architectural
gems

Population: 47.5 million
Languages: Uzbek, Tajik, Kyrgyz, Russian
Unit of currency: Uzbek som, Tajik somani, Kyrgyz som
How to get there: Turkish Airlines and Aeroflot link Central Asia to most of the world, while the growing fleets of local airlines Uzbekistan Airways and Air Astana serve a range of destinations across Eurasia. Some intrepid travellers enter the region overland from Iran, Russia or China.

'Any time I meet new people from Central Asia I'm touched by their friendliness and hospitality, which remains the same no matter where they live.'
-Gulmira Myrzakmat, Kyrgyzstan country director for the USAID CTJ project

TELL ME MORE...

These lands that wowed the likes of Ibn Battuta, Marco Polo and Chinggis (Genghis) Khan continue to impress, though for modern travellers it's significantly easier to get here. Between mud-brick oasis towns you'll pass through the imposing mountains of the Fann, Pamir, Alay and Tian Shan ranges, stopping along the way to trek to remote mountain lakes or enjoy the generous hospitality of local shepherd families and ride their horses to high-altitude panoramic passes. Improved national highway and railway systems make travel considerably faster and more comfortable than it was even five years ago – with the notable exception of the Pamir Highway – so getting to the end of the road and out into the wilderness has become much smoother. Combined with easier visas and more flight options, a trip through Central Asia is no longer the massive

ITINERARY
Three weeks on the Silk Road

● Wander **Khiva's** Ichon Qala, a museum-quality walled oasis city in the vast and inhospitable Kyzylkum desert.

● Marvel at the towering *medressas* of the Registan complex in **Samarkand**, once the heart of the powerful Timurid Empire.

● Dig into the 6000-year history of the **Sarazm** proto-urban archaeological site in Tajikistan's Zerafshan Valley.

● Loop through the Wakhan Corridor to gaze at Afghanistan's Hindu Kush mountains from the ramparts of **Yamchun Fort**, once an important Silk Road outpost.

● Combine a mini-pilgrimage climb of sacred Suleiman Too and classic Central Asian shopping at the Jayma Bazaar in Kyrgyzstan's second city, **Osh**.

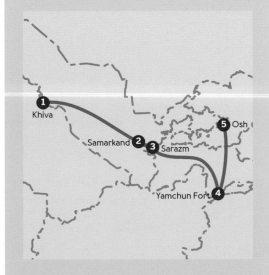

© MATTEO COLOMBO / GETTY IMAGES

Enjoy authentic local
hospitality in a Kyrgyz yurt

overland undertaking it was until very recently – unless, of course, you want it to be.

UNMISSABLE EXPERIENCES

● Watch the sun rise over the Registan's three monumental *medressas*, as nearby mosques sound the call to prayer and darkness yields to light above this centuries-old square.

● Silk Road–trip the Pamir Highway, which offers visitors insight into both the travails of travel in this rugged region and the remarkable pay-off in cultural riches and natural beauty that drew the likes of Marco Polo on his 1271 journey.

● Sleep in the *boz uy* yurts of the Kyrgyz nomads, who spend summers living a pastoralist

lifestyle their Silk Road ancestors would find intimately familiar.

TIME YOUR VISIT

Late spring (April) sees the snow-capped mountains of Tajikistan and Kyrgyzstan covered in wildflowers, and the deserts of Uzbekistan tolerably cool. Summer (June–August) is peak season for mountain hiking and horse-trekking but can be unbearably hot in the deserts. September is a great month to visit almost anywhere. Winter sports tourism is growing and kicks in at ski resorts from December, but outside of Kyrgyzstan expect mostly off-piste.

• By Stephen Lioy

Winding across remote high-altitude pastures, the Pamir Highway is one of the world's most spectacular roads

02

TOP 10 REGIONS

LE MARCHE, ITALY

It looks like the understudy is finally ready to take centre stage. Though the main roles usually go to its superstar neighbour, Tuscany, the Le Marche region of Italy has just as wide a repertoire. It can do higgledy-piggledy hilltop towns, gloriously gluttonous food festivals, resplendent Renaissance palaces, winding countryside and inviting beaches with equal panache, but with the added bonus that its attractions are much less well known. In 2020, the spotlight will shine brightly here as Urbino, Le Marche's most picturesque city, leads the celebrations to mark the 500th anniversary of the death of the great Renaissance painter – and local boy made good – Raphael.

The exquisite 15th-century city of Urbino

© STEFANO_VALERI / SHUTTERSTOCK

Population: 1.5 million

Main town: Ancona

Language: Italian

Unit of currency: Euro

How to get there: A limited number of international flights arrive at the Aeroporto delle Marche near Ancona. Far more serve Bologna, over 100km northwest of the region. Ferry services connect Ancona with Greece, Croatia and Turkey.

TELL ME MORE…

Exploring Le Marche's lesser-known treasures is like unlocking a secret level in the video game of Italy. Two-thirds of the region are hilly, albeit charmingly rather than intrepidly so, with no peak above 2500m. This up-and-down topography gives the landscape a pleasingly rumpled nature, like a patchwork quilt made of 50 shades of green, while its compact dimensions mean there are opportunities for sunbathing and skiing less than 50km apart (at different times of year, of course). In between – and often on top of – the hills are many of the splendidly ornate, elegantly weathered towns that Italy does so well where the museums are filled with old masters and the shops packed with salamis – a local delicacy. Tourism is still fairly low-key here but developing nicely with the emphasis placed firmly on sustainability, and the south of

Stalagtites and stalacmites fill the limestone caverns of the Grotte di Frasassi

© ADWO / SHUTTERSTOCK

The Furlo Gorge rises steeply alongside the bright green water of the Candigliano River

© LAURADIBIASE / GETTY IMAGES

ITINERARY
One week in Le Marche

● Explore the quirky museums – dedicated to handmade paper, bicycles, pianos and art – of **Fabriano**, a Unesco 'creative city'.

● Uncover the secrets of the Caesars along a stretch of the ancient Via Flaminia between **Pontericcioli** and **Fano** by way of the spectacular **Furlo Gorge**, taking in Roman bridges, tunnels and buildings en route.

● Wend your way down Le Marche's coast to the (often free) white-pebble beaches of **Sirolo** and inland forests of the adjacent Parco del Conero.

● Admire how **Ascoli Piceno** has bounced back after the 2016 earthquakes with a bowl of *olive all'ascolana* (deep-fried stuffed olives) in the city's almost impossibly elegant central square.

- 4 Fano
- 3 Furlo Gorge
- 2 Pontericcioli
- 1 Fabriano
- 5 Sirolo
- Ascoli Piceno 6

'Ascoli Piceno is a fine city with a ducal palace, museums and art galleries. Good for walking and embracing Italian street life, it looks how Italian cities are supposed to look.'
–Charles Mitchell, artist, Montevecchio, Province of Pesaro & Urbino

the region has (mostly) recovered well from the devastating earthquakes of 2016.

UNMISSABLE EXPERIENCES

● Train your eyes on the Renaissance art and your thighs on the scenic slopes of Urbino, a wondrous (and wondrously steep) 15th-century city and Unesco World Heritage Site.

● Admire the spelunking splendour of the Grotte di Frasassi, one of Europe's largest cave systems, a great mass of caverns and gnarly, dripping rock formations that somehow remained undiscovered until 1971.

● Go wildlife-spotting for bears, wolves and golden eagles amid the craggy mountains, wildflower meadows and sprawling forests of the Parco Nazionale dei Monti Sibillini, one of the few places in central Italy that still feels properly wild.

TIME YOUR VISIT

April to September brings the finest weather and coincides with numerous festivals: opera in Macerata (July to August) and Pesaro (August); jazz in Fano (July); and fried stuffed olives (!) in Ascoli di Piceno in April and May. Throughout 2020 there will be events and exhibitions in Urbino celebrating Raphael.

• By Joe Fullman

TOP 10 REGIONS

TŌHOKU, JAPAN

■■■■ **Japan will be buzzing in** 2020 as the world descends on Tokyo for the Summer Olympics, and perhaps no region in the country is more eager to get in on the party than Tōhoku. In recovery mode since the devastation of the 2011 earthquake and tsunami, this under-touristed swathe of the country has also been hard at work reopening transport links, developing new long-distance hiking trails, and rebuilding and improving tourist facilities. Already known within Japan for its dramatic natural landscapes, cultural heritage, historic festivals, good food and warm welcome, Tōhoku is emerging as a breath of fresh air for the crowd-weary adventurous visitor, and is just a few bullet-train hours northeast of the capital.

Towada-ko is a large caldera lake created by volcanic eruption

'Tōhoku hospitality is the best, and I love the outdoors, especially the coastal Kitayamazaki Cliffs and Ryūsendō Cave. Tōhoku really is the ideal blend of Japanese culture and nature.'

-Koichi Matsuda, lifelong Iwate resident

Population: 8.9 million

Main town: Sendai

Language: Japanese

Unit of currency: Japanese yen

How to get there: Tōhoku is linked to Tokyo by shinkansen (bullet train), which stops at hub cities Sendai, Morioka and Aomori. Sendai has the largest airport, serving mostly domestic flights.

TELL ME MORE...

The six prefectures of Tōhoku are defined by stunning natural features: mountain ranges, beech forests, volcanic peaks and caldera lakes make it a prime hiking, onsen-soaking and getting-away-from-it-all destination. Come winter, the landscape transforms into excellent skiing country. To the east is the Sanriku Coast, with sheer cliffs and jagged inlets, the new 700km Michinoku Coastal Trail, sandy bays, and small fishing ports – inspiring tsunami-affected communities that continue to rebuild. In 2019 the central stretch of the Rias train line finally reopened here, connecting north and south lines to create a 160km train journey along the Pacific.

Well-preserved former samurai districts and 12th-century temples are among the highlights in the towns. Meanwhile, Tōhoku breweries produce perhaps the country's (and the world's) finest sake.

It may not have the tourism polish of Tokyo

A monorail winds through the cherry blossom at Funaoka Castle Park, Sendai

© BULE SKY STUDIO / SHUTTERSTOCK

(or the overcrowding), but Tōhoku is the place for slow, off-the-beaten-path travel and uncontrived local experiences – and did we mention the sake?

UNMISSABLE EXPERIENCES

● Indulge in a much-loved Japanese pastime with a soak in an onsen. Numerous onsen are dotted throughout the region: choose from a collection of baths in forested surrounds at Nyūtō Onsen village; or head to ski town Zaō Onsen to bathe with dozens of new naked friends in the large *rotemburo* (outdoor bath) below the mountain.

● Take the *wanko-soba* challenge: how many small servings of noodles can you quickly slurp

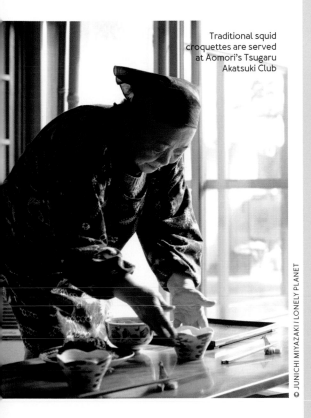

Traditional squid croquettes are served at Aomori's Tsugaru Akatsuki Club

© JUNICHI MIYAZAKI / LONELY PLANET

ITINERARY
Ten days in Tōhoku

● Explore former feudal-era capital **Aizu-Wakamatsu**, home to some of the region's best sake breweries.

● Stay in lively **Sendai** for trips to the island-dotted bay of Matsushima and mountain temples of Yamadera.

● Visit the Buddhist sites and gardens surrounding Unesco World Heritage town **Hiraizumi**.

● Next take a scenic detour along the northern **Sanriku Coast** before heading to **Towada-ko** caldera lake for a hike or boat cruise.

● Go back in time in **Kakunodate** with a wander through its samurai district.

● Follow in the footsteps of pilgrims up the 2446 stone steps at Haguro-san, one of the three sacred peaks of **Dewa Sanzan**.

down, one after another, in one sitting? Try this 300-year-old tradition at restaurant Azumaya in Iwate Prefecture; you'll receive a plaque if you can manage 100 bowlfuls (surprisingly not uncommon!).

TIME YOUR VISIT

Every season has its appeal. Autumn colours are particularly stunning in November, and spring (March–May) draws crowds for cherry-blossom viewing. While snow may disrupt travel in winter, it also means magical landscapes and onsen appreciation. In summer (June–August), Tōhoku hosts some of Japan's best festivals. The Tokyo Olympics run from 24 July to 9 August.

• By Laura Crawford

5 Towada-ko

4 Sanriku Coast

Kakunodate 6

3 Hiraizumi

Dewa Sanzan 7

2 Sendai

Aizu-Wakamatsu 1

Kitayamazaki Cliffs on the
dramatic Sanriku Coast

04

MAINE, USA

New England's biggest state has always been full of pride, but this year the love for 'Vacationland' will reach fever pitch as Maine celebrates its bicentennial. Across the region, towns and cities are holding special exhibitions, concerts and festivals to commemorate 200 years of statehood. Of course, even if Maine wasn't celebrating a major milestone, it would still be a great time to visit. The culinary scene has exploded in recent years, and you'll find farm-to-table restaurants, coffee roasters, artisanal bakers and craft brewers all across the state. And despite Maine's growing popularity, it's easy to escape the crowds amid the state's vast forests and its dramatic, lighthouse-strewn coastline.

A lighthouse guards Bass Harbor in Acadia National Park

© APPALACHIANVIEWS / GETTY IMAGES

Population: 1.3 million
Main town: Portland
Language: English
Unit of currency: US dollar
How to get there: Portland International Jetport offers mostly domestic flights to cities on the East Coast. Boston Logan airport has international connections, and it's just over an hour's drive to Maine's southern border.

'Living in Maine is a choice to stay fully connected to primal rhythms — seasons, cycles, your own creativity, your own intellectual calling, to wildness and to full responsibility for your life.'
-Johanna Barrett, former globetrotter and owner of Compass Rose Books in Castine

TELL ME MORE...
Maine has a dazzling array of natural wonders. In Acadia National Park, the mountains meet the sea in a pristine landscape of forests, wave-kissed shores and rocky promontories offering dramatic sunrise vistas. Way up north, the vast moose-filled wilderness of Baxter State Park draws outdoor lovers who come for canoeing on misty lakes and challenging scrambles up Maine's craggy summits. There's also white-water rafting on thundering rivers, sea kayaking the vast island-studded bays and multi-day sailing trips on vintage masted ships. Maine also has plenty of spots for more easy-going adventures, whether digging your feet in the sand at Ogunquit and other pretty beaches in the south, or catching the ferry out to a remote island for a day of exploring sea cliffs and flower-filled meadows. And then there's

ITINERARY
One week in Maine

● Take in the waterfront views, then stroll the cobblestone streets of **Portland**'s Old Port district. Finish with dinner and drinks at Vinland, serving 100% locally sourced organic cuisine.
● Wander through the sun-dappled trails of the **Coastal Maine Botanical Gardens**, a beautiful reserve of forest, meadow and ornamental gardens.
● Admire the coastline on a sailing or kayaking adventure out of **Rockland**. Afterwards, stretch your legs on the seaside walk out to Rockland Breakwater Lighthouse.
● Take in the panoramic views after hiking to the top of **Cadillac Mountain** in Acadia National Park, then recharge over tea and popovers (hollow pastries served with jam) at **Jordan Pond House**.

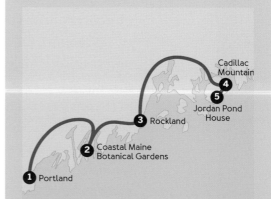

The classic Maine lobster roll tastes like summer

the lobster. Seafood shacks dot the length of Maine's coastline and provide the perfect setting for an unforgettable feast.

UNMISSABLE EXPERIENCES

● One of the best places to experience Maine's rugged wilderness, Baxter State Park offers more than 320km of hiking trails, among mountains, streams and lakes. Some of Maine's highest peaks are here, including Mt Katahdin, the fabled end point for the 3500km Appalachian Trail.

● Unplug from the 21st-century on Monhegan, a small rocky island 16km off the coast of Maine. With a year-round population in the double digits and gorgeous clifftop hikes, Monhegan feels like a throwback to another time. Visit on a day trip from Clyde, or better yet, spend the night in one of the simple island inns.

TIME YOUR VISIT

Maine's high summer season, which runs from June to August, offers ideal weather for seaside frolics and outdoor adventures (hiking, rafting, sailing). The summer also brings a packed lineup of food and arts festivals, plus old-fashioned country fairs. Autumn blazes light up the forest from late September to early October — a magical time for a road trip.

• By Regis St Louis

TOP 10 REGIONS

LORD HOWE ISLAND, AUSTRALIA

Parked in the middle of nowhere 600km off the Australian coast, this visually stunning island makes an instant impact on the senses with its jaw-dropping World Heritage–listed beauty. Two soaring green mountains overlook a perfect lagoon and the world's southernmost coral reef; perfect crescents of beach and splendid hiking trails through the lush forest add to brilliant outdoors possibilities. This onetime volcano's isolation makes it a refuge for many endemic species, as well as plentiful birdlife. The island is a shining example of sustainably managed tourism; only 400 visitors are allowed at any time, and you are encouraged to participate in a series of ecological projects. Lord Howe's remoteness and manageable size make it an idyllic escape.

05

Lord Howe's
mountains rise
from the lagoon

Lord Howe kingfish are a drawcard for anglers

© EPSTOCK / SHUTTERSTOCK

Population: 400
Language: English
Unit of currency: Australian dollar
How to get there: Daily Qantaslink flights from Sydney or weekend flights from Brisbane.

TELL ME MORE...

You can leave your phone in flight mode when you arrive…there's no network. Enjoy the digital detox and relax into the pace of island life. Need to make a call? Find a payphone (remember those?). But don't relax too much: there's so much to do here. The diving is world class, with amazingly clear water offering visibility that is regularly 30 to 40m. Hikes offer special views throughout, but none better than from the guided ascent of Mt Gower, one of two muscular peaks that dominate the whole island.

Lord Howe's isolation has endowed it with a unique ecology, with many plant and insect species found only here. Birdlife is a highlight, with raucously nesting terns and the eerie cries of muttonbirds in their burrows punctuating the night. Ecological projects are underway to eliminate all non-native species and you can participate in scientific surveys of various wildlife populations during your stay on the island.

UNMISSABLE EXPERIENCES

● Take a guided hike up Mt Gower. This eight- to ten-hour return walk will reward with astounding views from the 875m summit as well as great insight into the island from the guide.

● Jump on a boat trip to Ball's Pyramid. This soaring, spine-tinglingly jagged crag rises vertically over 500m out of the ocean. There's brilliant birdwatching and diving here, some 23km southeast of Lord Howe.

● Dine at the Anchorage restaurant. The island's best place to eat is a convivial spot at any time of day but is especially appealing in the evening. Kingfish (yellowtail amberjack) is a delicious meal, sustainably caught locally.

A boat trip to striking Ball's Pyramid is a memorable experience

© SOUTHERN LIGHTSCAPES-AUSTRALIA | GETTY IMAGES

'Lord Howe is famous for pristine coral gardens, lush forests, big mountains and rare birds. However, the real attraction is its friendly, relaxed vibe and the complete disconnect from your day-to-day life.'

-Dani Rourke, director, Pinetrees Lodge

TIME YOUR VISIT

Visitor numbers are restricted; trips must be planned ahead. Domestic tourists visit in quantity from December to February, when accommodation rates are sky-high. Visiting off-season can be more rewarding. The best birdwatching is September to November, while diving season runs right from September through to June. Winter (June to August) temperatures are pleasant and accommodation is at its cheapest.

• By Andy Symington

ITINERARY
Five days on Lord Howe Island

● Get into holiday mode with gentle walking and beach exploration. Snorkel at **Ned's Beach** and head up to **Kim's Lookout**.

● Ascend majestic **Mt Gower** with a guide. It's a long climb, but you won't need any special skills.

● Go diving at one of 60 excellent dive sites. With experience, head to unforgettable **Ball's Pyramid**.

● Explore the lagoon on a leisurely turtle-spotting boat trip or grab a kayak and paddle to idyllic **North Beach** for a picnic.

● Booking in a spare day pays: diving and Mt Gower are weather-dependent. Otherwise, climb up **Intermediate Hill** and down via the slopes of Mt Lidgbird.

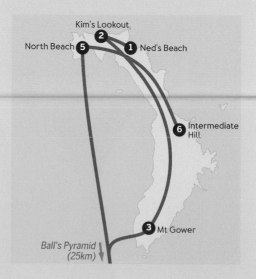

Kim's Lookout
2
North Beach **5**   **1** Ned's Beach
6 Intermediate Hill
3 Mt Gower
Ball's Pyramid (25km)

TOP 10 REGIONS

GUIZHOU PROVINCE, CHINA

Guizhou is a province on the cusp. Its capital, Guiyang, is a city of more than 4 million (that's greater than the city-limit populations of LA, Rome and Berlin). Streets brim with street-food stalls come evening, and a bowl of spicy rice noodles costs pennies, but down back alleyways, artisan businesses, cafes and craft bars are starting to open. In the countryside, teetery wooden villages still linger almost unchanged for centuries, but have begun to develop traveller amenities. All of this is connected by new high-speed rail lines, meaning you can zip to Chongqing or Kunming from Guiyang in a couple of hours. And China's ongoing engineering efforts have resulted in gleaming new highways and bridges that make getting into and around Guizhou's mystical mountains a 21st-century effort.

he ancient city
of Zhenyuan on
he banks of the
Wuyang River

© 4045 / SHUTTERSTOCK

'Guizhou is a simple, natural and beautiful place. I work creating opportunities for women batik and embroidery artists from the Miao culture, and admire how deep and rich the traditions of the minority cultures here are.'

-Yu Ying, founder of Village Story artisan workshop

Population: 35 million
Main town: Guiyang
Language: Mandarin Chinese
Unit of currency: Renminbi
How to get there: Guiyang airport serves flights across mainland China and regional international flights. High-speed rail services connect Guiyang and a handful of smaller cities to neighbouring Yunnan, Guangxi and Sichuan and further afield in China. Regional bus and train services help you get around; hiring a driver is recommended to reach some of the province's most rural areas and small villages.

TELL ME MORE…

Remote Guizhou is largely unknown to modern travellers, though it was once a main artery on the Tea-Horse Road trading route between ancient China and the Tibetan plateau. Guizhou stayed secreted away, its tiny wooden villages left untouched in the province's signature misty mountains.

Change began a few years ago, when impoverished Guizhou became a technological destination of choice – such companies as Apple, Huawei and Tencent began moving in to take advantage of the province's cool year-round climate for big data storage. In 2016, the world's largest filled-aperture radio telescope, FAST, began receiving transmissions here with the hope of finding life on other planets (though it's normally closed to visitors).

Guizhou is home to more of China's recognised ethnic minority groups than any other province, including the Miao and Dong cultures. Investment has led to the development of local villages, where beautifully rendered boutique inns now offer rooms with views of rice paddies, and it's still possible to gain an understanding of an ancient way of life while also enjoying modern amenities.

Social enterprises have also started. Danzhai Wanda Village – a charitable resort opened in 2017 – was designed to create space for minority artists and craftspeople to showcase their works to visitors, thereby bringing new jobs to locals.

UNMISSABLE EXPERIENCES

● As Guizhou is home to many ethnic minority groups, villages of all stripes dot the mountains here. In Zhaoxing, you can get a feeling for how life carries on more or less as it always has, but with added traveller comforts such as charming cafes and pretty hotels.

● The town of Zhenyuan was a county capital as early as 202 BC and a Tea-Horse Road trading outpost. Its sublime riverside location and ancient temples provide the perfect antidote to hyper-modern China.

● Guizhou abounds in natural wonders – most travellers head straight to stunning Huangguoshu Falls, but you can explore monkey-filled mountains in capital city Guiyang's Qianlingshan Park if you're short on time.

TIME YOUR VISIT

Guizhou's cool climate is one of its drawcards (for Big Data and tourists), meaning it's possible

A covered 'wind and rain' bridge shelters Dong villagers in Zhaoxing

ITINERARY
One week in Guizhou Province

● From capital city Guiyang, head to Anshun where you can hike up to the ethereal Rhinoceros Pool and witness the misty cascade of **Huangguoshu Falls**, Guizhou's most beloved natural attraction.

● Explore uplit stalagmites and icicle-shaped rock formations inside **Zhijin Cave**, China's largest cave.

● Head to **Danzhai** to learn about the local Miao and Dong cultures in the nearby villages of Xijiang and Zhaoxing.

● Wander Sifangjing Xiang, a collection of photogenic, cluttered alleyways lined with wooden inns and otherworldly dead-ends in the riverside village of **Zhenyuan**.

● Discover the deep gorges and surreal red sandstone cliffs that make up the unusual geology around **Chishui**.

© PIDJOE// GETTY IMAGES

5 Chishui

Zhenyuan **4**

Zhijin Cave
2

3 Danzhai

1 Huangguoshu Falls

to visit through China's normally unbearable summer (June–August). However, the most beautiful time of year to visit is late spring (April), when mountain blooms abound and waterfalls are at their most thunderous. In October and November, you can witness the traditional new year celebrations of the Miao culture in the ancient villages around Danzhai.

• By Megan Eaves

Huangguoshu Falls is the most impressive of many of the waterfalls and karst caves in the area

TOP 10 REGIONS

CÁDIZ PROVINCE, SPAIN

■■■■■ **With a string of gastronomic triumphs,** Cádiz province is wandering into the spotlight. Queen of the Sherry Triangle, Jerez de la Frontera welcomed its first Michelin star in 2018 courtesy of Juan Luis Fernández' restaurant Lú, Cocina y Alma, and its 20th-century *tabancos* have been rescued from extinction by enterprising new owners. Even sherry is fashionable again! In El Puerto de Santa María, Ángel León's Aponiente is one of just two three-Michelin-star restaurants in Andalucía. Hot on its heels is León's one-starred Alevante in Sancti Petri. Vejer de la Frontera has recast itself as a foodie and boutique-hotel hub, and up-to-the-minute cafes, restaurants and accommodation are breathing fresh energy into Phoenician-origin Cádiz. Throw in new flights to Jerez and this region is ripe for discovery.

© KAVALENKAVA / SHUTTERSTOCK

The Catedral de Cádiz rises above the rooftops of the city

Population: 1.2 million

Main town: Cádiz

Language: Spanish

Unit of currency: Euro

How to get there: Jerez, the only airport in Cádiz province, is served by a growing number of flights to/from destinations across Europe. You can also fly into Seville, an hour's drive or train from Jerez, or into Gibraltar, then hop across the Spanish border into Cádiz.

TELL ME MORE...

Enamoured travellers return time and again to Spain's southernmost province. Is it the glugs of dry sherry on a Cádiz backstreet? The flutter of palms on Vejer's tile-adorned plaza? The thrill of a hike up 1648m El Torreón in the beautifully rugged Parque Natural Sierra de Grazalema? The warmth of the *gaditanos* and

'You never get used to Cádiz' beauty: gazing out on the Atlantic from Vejer, immersing yourself in nature in Santa Lucía, lunching at Las Rejas opposite the Roman ruins on Bolonia beach... These are our everyday privileges.'

–Eugenia Claver, owner of boutique hotel La Fonda Antigua in Vejer de la Frontera

their limitless love for their homeland? All of it, no doubt, and more. Jerez – capital of sherry, horses and (dare we say it?) flamenco – has long been an under-the-radar, rough-around-the-edges jewel of Andalucía and the wind-lashed Costa de la Luz a blissfully undeveloped beach escape, but the freshly blooming local-inspired, local-ingredient culinary scene has put the entire province on the map. Cookery prowess

Bodegas Tradición is one of Jerez' most intriguing sherry bodegas

A traditional Andalucian house with a shrine to the Virgin in Vejer de la Frontera

© YADID LEVY / LONELY PLANET

© JUAN ANTONIO ORIHUELA / SHUTTERSTOCK

ITINERARY
Two weeks in Cádiz province

● Start in **Jerez de la Frontera** at Bodegas Tradición – sipping extra-aged sherries among paintings by such greats as Goya, El Greco and Zurbarán, before catching some flamenco at Tabanco El Pasaje.

● Visit cliff-hugging **Arcos de la Frontera** en route to the **Parque Natural Sierra de Grazalema**, then go kayaking, canyoning, caving and paragliding, and hike the **Garganta Verde**.

● Take a kitesurfing class in barefoot-boho **Tarifa**, before enjoying the seductive salt-white beaches and **Bolonia**'s Roman ruins.

● Dive into the food scene of **Vejer de la Frontera** with a cooking course at Annie B's and wander the sun-bleached streets while staying at an Andalucía-chic boutique hideaway.

● Visit the baroque-neoclassical cathedral, white-gold beaches and Barrio de la Viña (the city's Carnaval epicentre) in joyful **Cádiz**.

aside, a blossoming wellness vibe is sweeping along the Costa de la Luz, and Cádiz invites as it always has done, with its riotous mid-February Carnaval, its unspoilt natural spaces and its hauntingly beautiful fortified white towns, which once watched over the turbulent Moorish-Christian frontier.

UNMISSABLE EXPERIENCES

● Centuries-old bodegas, handsome Andalucian horses, a mighty 11th- or 12th-century Almohad *alcázar* (castle) and earthy *tabancos* hosting soul-stirringly authentic flamenco are the key appeals of sherry-loving Jerez de la Frontera.

● It's all about wandering the distinctive, history-rich *barrios* (districts), gorging on fried fish, seeking out spontaneous flamenco and drinking in the bubbly atmosphere in famously cheerful capital Cádiz – Europe's oldest continuously inhabited settlement, founded in 1100 BC by the Phoenicians.

● No Cádiz trip is complete without lazing away a few days (or weeks) on the wild, windswept Costa de la Luz, with its ravishing blonde beaches, blissful boutique hotels and lively kitesurfing scene.

TIME YOUR VISIT

April, May, June, September and October are typically the top months weather-wise. Spring sees a flurry of festivals, including Jerez' Feria del Caballo. Crowds peak in July/August, especially on the Costa de la Luz, but quieter September remains beach-day warm. May, June and September are perfect for kitesurfing/ windsurfing and hiking (also good in October).

• By Isabella Noble

Kitesurfing is popular
on Tarifa's Playa de los
Lances

08

The booming
spectacle of
Iguazú Falls, the
planet's largest
waterfall
system

08
BEST IN
TRAVEL
2020

NORTHEAST ARGENTINA

With South America's most impressive falls, a rich regional history and exceptional wildlife watching, Northeast Argentina should be on everyone's list. Of course there's the famous Iguazú, one of the seven natural wonders of the world, but the rest of this rugged and temperate region will lead you well off the beaten path. Newly minted in 2018, Iberá National Park is poised to become one of Argentina's greatest attractions. It's an inspiring success story of how restoring wilderness can have a positive impact on adjacent communities. Rewilding is bringing back the native fauna, from the green-winged macaw to pampas deer and jaguars. Also, the country continues to be great value for travellers.

Population: 3.7 million
Main towns: Puerto Iguazú, Mercedes, Corrientes
Language: Spanish
Unit of currency: Argentine peso
How to get there: From Buenos Aires, flights go to Puerto Iguazú, Corrientes and Resistencia; comfortable overnight buses link Mercedes to the capital.

'I love getting out early to see the daybreak from a canoe. You can watch swamp deer and caimans sunning themselves, and clouds or brilliant sun reflected in calm waters.'

-Ariadna MacNab, community tourism coordinator

TELL ME MORE...

With the recent creation of Iberá National Park, one of South America's principal freshwater wetlands also became Argentina's largest protected area. Think South American safari: this watery expanse is a haven for wildlife. Camp among docile capybaras, ply through lily-choked waters to spy prehistoric-looking caimans and spot herds of rheas and flocks of reintroduced green-tipped macaws. Native jaguars and giant river otters are coming back, thanks to an innovative rewilding program based in the remote island outpost of San Alonso. Take in the region's *gaucho* routes with a horseback-riding tour and admire the barefoot cowboys and banner-blue skies. In between excursions, soak up the slow pace of such colonial towns as Concepción and Colonia Pellegrini. While checking out the larger-than-life landscape of Iguazú Falls, explore the steamy subtropical forest of Misiones, stay at a jungle lodge in Puerto Iguazú, and visit the fascinating ruins of early Jesuit missions.

ITINERARY
One week in Northeast Argentina

● Soak up the spray of **Iguazú Falls** on the maze of boardwalks leading to jaw-dropping viewpoints. Plan an extra day to explore the Brazilian side.

● Explore the Jesuit Mission ruins of **San Ignacio Miní** for insight into the clash that colonisation brought to indigenous life here.

● Use the time-forgotten village of **Colonia Pellegrini** as your base for excursions into **Iberá National Park**, boating the estuary to see great numbers of caimans, swamp deer and diverse birdlife.

● Explore **Rincón del Socorro** for a taste of *estancia* (ranch) life among huge populations of rheas, native deer and capybaras (the world's largest rodents).

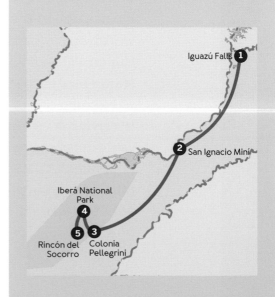

A caiman watches roseate spoonbills take flight in Iberá National Park

UNMISSABLE EXPERIENCES

Outside Concepción, travel via horse-drawn canoe to traditional settlements on tiny islands in the estuary. Canoes ply through shallow waters surrounded by fragrant water lilies and abundant birdlife. Once used for cattle operations, the islands were home to a thousand residents ranching in this watery world; today there are only thirty. A similar program lets you both ride and swim with the horses, which have become well adapted to their aquatic environment. A community partnership with the Conservation Land Trust created these unique tours to preserve this fading way of life. In turn, rural residents are finding new opportunities and reasons to stay.

TIME YOUR VISIT

Avoid the summer months of December to February when temperatures soar above the comfort zone. Cool and dry, August can be favourable for wildlife watching, as water sources have somewhat dried up. September and October are prime months to visit Iguazú if you want to avoid the crowds.

• By Carolyn McCarthy

TOP 10 REGIONS

KVARNER GULF, CROATIA

◼◼◼◼ Sandwiched between the tourist hotspots of Dalmatia and Istria, this less heralded part of the Croatian coast has been quietly building up its credentials in the culinary and environmental-protection spheres over the last decade. Now the Kvarner Gulf is well and truly ready for its close up, with its principal settlement, the gritty port city of Rijeka, embracing the role of European Capital of Culture in 2020. Shiny new set pieces include architecturally repurposed spaces for museums and cultural centres. In supporting roles but ready to steal the show are the gulf islands, with their ageless beauty, historic walled towns replete with Venetian-era architecture, numerous beaches and considerable charm.

Baška's pebble beach on Krk Island awaits bathers

© ANDREW MAYOVSKYY | SHUTTERSTOCK

Population: 296,000
Main town: Rijeka
Language: Croatian
Unit of currency: Kuna

How to get there: Rijeka Airport is on the island of Krk, 30km from the city, but it's only used for seasonal flights in the warmer months. Rijeka is connected to Zagreb and Ljubljana by train, and coaches head here from all over Croatia and neighbouring countries.

TELL ME MORE...

Rijeka may not be the prettiest but it's proud of its reputation as conservative Croatia's most liberal city, turning out some of the country's edgiest bands and heralding itself as a 'Port

'Rijeka is an open, tolerant, vibrant city, which is searching for a way out of its industrial past. This process is creative and you can feel it.'

-Andro Stošić, manager of Dharma Hostel

of Diversity'. Up the coast, the humble fishing village of Volosko and historic hill town of Kastav are evolving as culinary hotspots – benefiting from the top-notch truffles, olive oils and wines of neighbouring Istria, and combining them with the Kvarner's own flavoursome seafood and herb-grazed lamb.

The large gulf islands of Rab, Krk, Lošinj and Cres offer the usual Croatian cocktail of historic walled towns, ancient ruins, crystal-clear waters and popular beaches. The waters to the east of Lošinj and Cres are a protected marine reserve, with a resident population of bottlenose dolphins and sea turtles. Meanwhile, bears, wolves and lynxes still lurk in forgotten corners of Risnjak National Park and Učka Nature Park on the mainland.

UNMISSABLE EXPERIENCES

● Explore the narrow lanes at the ancient core of Rab, the main settlement on the island of

A climber scales a limestone tower in Učka Nature Park

© MELLOWMESHER / SHUTTERSTOCK

ITINERARY
Ten days in the Kvarner Gulf

● Start in **Rijeka**, using it as a base to visit Kastav, Volosko, the Austro-Hungarian resort town of Opatija and **Učka Nature Park**.

● Take the Brestova–Porozina ferry to **Cres** and stop to explore Venetian-era Cres Town en route to cute **Osor**.

● Continue over the bridge to Lošinj and head for the pretty harbour town of **Mali Lošinj**.

● Backtrack and catch the Merag–Valbiska ferry to **Krk**; set aside a full day to drive around the island.

● Take the Valbiska–Lopar ferry to **Rab**, and base yourself in Rab Town for the remainder of your stay.

the same name. Punctuated by four distinctive Venetian church towers, it's the Kvarner's prettiest walled town. Other contenders include Osor, Cres Town and Krk Town.

● Feast on fine regional cuisine at Kukuriku in the atmospheric hilltop town of Kastav. There are further excellent options down by the seaside in Volosko.

● Book a day tour with the rangers in Učka Nature Park, keeping an eye out for bears as you take in the scenery of the Kvarner's high country.

TIME YOUR VISIT
Rijeka kicks off its stint as 2020 European Capital of Culture with its famous annual pre-Lenten Carnival on 23 February. The warmer weather kicks in around May and lingers until October; avoid the school-holiday crowds in July and August and start planning for the shoulder season instead.

• By Peter Dragicevich

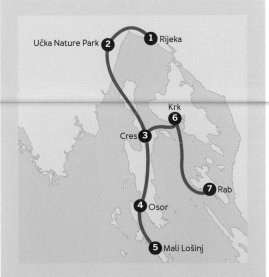

Učka Nature Park ② — ① Rijeka
Krk ⑥
Cres ③
⑦ Rab
④ Osor
⑤ Mali Lošinj

BRAZILIAN AMAZON

The Brazilian Amazon is the natural world at its purest – an ancient place that, with its polychromatic wildlife and chaotic, knotted flora, seems practically hallucinogenic. This misty jungle is home to some of the world's rarest plants and animals, as well as communities that have remained stewards of this great green expanse for centuries. As our planet's climate shifts, conservation of the Brazilian Amazon has become paramount. In 2020, thoughtful and well-planned travel to the most important forest on earth will support sustainable travel efforts, simultaneously benefiting local communities and the national economy, and highlighting the cultural and monetary value in preservation.

Early morning fog over the Amazon River

Population: 17 million

Main towns: Belém, Manaus, Santarém

Languages: Portuguese, indigenous Amazonian languages

Unit of currency: Brazilian real

How to get there: The primary (and fastest) way to access the Brazilian Amazon is by air. The major transport hubs are Belém and Manaus – both host frequent domestic flights and Manaus has international air services. These cities are also accessible by car or bus, though road conditions around Manaus can be unpredictable. Boat travel on the river is also possible, though travel times between cities are long.

TELL ME MORE...

In a word, the Brazilian Amazon is massive. It spans seven states, the largest of which can fit France inside three times over. Within this

'Living and working in a preserved area of the Amazon is a sensorial experience. I can find the best of everything: freshwater streams, pristine jungle, organic papaya and salad leaves from my garden.'

-Vanessa Mariño, owner of Amazon Emotions Lodge

space, rivers of all kinds – hot and cold, muddy and clear, big and small – crisscross an arboreal network full of nature's obvious and not-so-obvious wonders to meet the region's namesake waterway, a behemoth aquatic thoroughfare that stretches a whopping 6400km. Brazil is home to 60% of the entire Amazon rainforest, and its effect on the country's cultural, environmental and economic history is profound.

Jaguars are a rare but rewarding wildlife spot in the Brazilian Amazon

© MARKTUCAN / SHUTTERSTOCK

ITINERARY
Three to four weeks in the Brazilian Amazon

● Start in **Manaus,** exploring the city and taking trips to wildlife-rich **Rio Urubu** and the caves and waterfalls of **Presidente Figueiredo.**

● Continue to Tefé (either by flight or boat journey) to explore the **Mamirauá Reserve,** renowned for its sustainable environmental and cultural practices. You might catch a glimpse of a treetop-dwelling jaguar.

● Head back to Manaus and take a riverboat to Novo Airão, the jumping-off point for tours to **Reserva Extrativista Baixo Rio Branco-Jauaperi,** one of the best places to spot wildlife.

● Take a riverboat to Santarém and scoot out to **Floresta Nacional do Tapajós** to walk around the buttressed roots of the huge samaúma trees. Stop in Alter do Chão for some R & R.

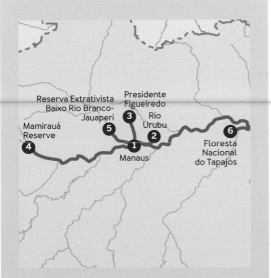

The experience of wandering this ecological Eden is worth the effort to get there – ascend climbing lines to recline in the treetops with the macaws, kayak along the glassy waters with river dolphins, or hike across the forest floor to spot a kaleidoscope of tiny treefrogs.

Millions of people live here in communities ranging from the bustling cities of Manaus and Belém to small riverside hamlets. Meeting them is an essential part of visiting this vital region of the country.

UNMISSABLE EXPERIENCES
● Spot the red-faced white uakari monkey in the treetops of the Mamirauá Reserve, Brazil's largest intact *várzea* (seasonally flooded rainforest) – this animal is found nowhere else in the world. Visit the reserve in the months following rainy season to glide through the partially submerged trees by canoe.

● Lounge on the beaches of Ilha do Amor, the paradisiacal island near Alter do Chão, a congenial riverside town. When you're not relaxing on the glistening sand or tucking into a plate of *pirarucú àmoda de casa* at the waterfront restaurants, hit the nearby lagoon for stand-up paddleboarding.

TIME YOUR VISIT
The dry season runs from June to December – things warm up and the hiking trails are at their most accessible. The wet season spans January to May and during this time water levels rise significantly, allowing for flooded forest exploration via boat. That said, prepare to get wet and for some impeded road travel.

• By Bailey Freeman

TOP 10 CITIES

Salzburg, Austria / Washington, DC, USA / Cairo, Egypt
Galway, Ireland / Bonn, Germany / La Paz, Bolivia / Kochi, India
Vancouver, Canada / Dubai, UAE / Denver, USA

SALZBURG, AUSTRIA

Drumroll, please: the Salzburg Festival is turning 100, and this heart-stealer of an Alpine city is singing about it at the top of its voice. One of the world's greatest classical music shindigs, the festival is always a riotous feast of opera, classical music and drama – and never more so than in 2020. Salzburg will be pulling out all the stops for the centenary, with special exhibitions and events taking place all over the historic centre – concerts, plays, readings, Mozart matinees, you name it. Top billing, as always, will go to Hugo von Hofmannsthal's *Jedermann*, based on a medieval morality play and performed in all its glory in Domplatz. So dust off your dirndl or lederhosen, book your tickets months ahead, and get ready to rock into the summer like Amadeus (perhaps minus the wig).

© JAKOBRADLGRUBER/GETTY IMAGES

The mighty fortress of Festung Hohensalzburg overlooks the city

01

Population: 153,380
Languages: German
Unit of currency: Euro
How to get there: Salzburg International Airport, a 20-minute bus ride from the historic centre, has regular flights all over Europe. There are excellent rail connections with the rest of Austria and beyond from the Hauptbahnhof.

'I love Salzburg's contrasts – this is a city located right between the mountains and the flat country, with stylish urban living and enchanting landscapes. It's intimate, exciting and musically vibrant.'

-Andreas Gfrerer, chairman of City Marketing Salzburg

TELL ME MORE...

With a Unesco-listed baroque old town, a high-on-a-hill medieval fortress, galleries rammed with phenomenal art, some of Europe's finest concert halls and uplifting mountain views to make you want to yodel out loud, Salzburg never loses its touch. It's all dressed up and at its vibrant best when the Salzburg Festival comes to town for six weeks (from late July to August), bringing song, theatre and orchestral highs to such venues as the Grosses Festspielhaus, Felsenreitschule and cathedral-topped Domplatz.

Sitting astride the milky turquoise Salzach River, this city is where Mozart was born and bred, and where Maria made her warbling debut in *The Sound of Music*. If you're looking for a perfectly orchestrated Alpine city, this is it. To start at the very beginning, make for the historic lanes of the Altstadt, a triumph of baroque urban design, where the prince-archbishops, great patrons of the arts, once held court.

ITINERARY
Three days in Salzburg

● Boost your sightseeing stamina with a single-origin espresso at retro-cool **220GRAD** as the Altstadt begins to wake up.
● Hit **Residenzplatz** before the crowds descend. With its stately palace, Residenz, horse-drawn carriages and lavish fountain, the baroque plaza is Salzburg in a nutshell.
● Take the lift up to the **Museum der Moderne**. Check out the gallery's first-rate exhibitions of contemporary art, before a highly scenic woodland walk atop **Mönchsberg's** cliffs.
● Cross the river to opulent 17th-century **Schloss Mirabell**. The castle-view gardens are sublime. Return at 8pm for chamber concerts of Mozart's music in the frescoed Marble Hall.
● Raise a tankard beneath the chestnut trees in the 1000-seat beer garden of monastery-run brewery **Augustiner Bräustübl**.

UNMISSABLE EXPERIENCES

● Peer out across the Altstadt's domes, spires and rooftops on Festungsgasse, a balcony trail to Salzburg's cake-topper of a fortress, Hohensalzburg, built in 1077 to make the city impregnable to would-be invaders.

● Belt out 'Do-Re-Mi' and other *The Sound of Music* faves with a 3½-hour spin around movie locations with Fräulein Maria's Bicycle Tours. Stops include the Mirabellgarten, Benedictine Nonnberg Abbey and palaces Schloss Leopoldskron and Hellbrunn.

● Make a pilgrimage to the bright-yellow house on Getreidegasse where child prodigy Mozart was born in 1756. Highlights saluting the genius include the mini violin he played as a toddler.

TIME YOUR VISIT

In winter, Salzburg twinkles with Christmas-market cheer (December) and world-renowned orchestras strike up at Mozart Week (January). Room rates peak in summer, and advance planning is essential for the Salzburg Festival, with tickets selling like hot cakes. Spring and autumn are often mild, with fewer crowds and better deals.

• By Kerry Walker

Strauss' opera *Salome* performed at the Salzburg Festival

© SALZBURGER FESTSPIELE / RUTH WALZ

The lavish 17th-century Schloss Mirabell overlooks its elegant formal gardens

02
BEST IN
TRAVEL
2020

WASHINGTON, DC, USA

All eyes will be on Washington, DC, this year, as the city celebrates the 100th anniversary of the 19th Amendment – the law that granted women the right to vote. Iconic museums like the National Portrait Gallery, the National Museum of American History and the National Museum of Women in the Arts will have special exhibitions related to this major milestone in human rights. Tie this in to the excitement for this year's presidential election and DC will be one of America's most dynamic cities in 2020. Politics aside, Washington's renaissance is in full bloom, with a revitalised waterfront, celebrated new museums and an exploding food scene. Sustainability remains everyone's favourite topic, and the city is looking greener than ever.

On the bank of the Tidal Basin, the Jefferson Memorial honours the third US president

© SHARKSHOCK / SHUTTERSTOCK

Population: 703,000
Language: English
Unit of currency: US dollar
How to get there: It's easy to reach DC, with three major airports serving the city: Dulles International, Ronald Reagan Washington National and BWI Marshall Airport.

TELL ME MORE...

Once neglected neighbourhoods are suddenly on the rise, with revitalised spaces that have drawn a new wave of restaurateurs, microbrewers and craft makers. One riverfront stretch of Southwest DC has been reborn as the Wharf, home to over 20 new restaurants, several live music venues and a rum distillery. You can hire kayaks for a paddle along Washington Channel or stroll the waterfront, checking out the neighbourhood's new

sustainable features (green roofs, hundreds of newly planted trees and an innovative floating wetlands system). Further upriver, the world-renowned Kennedy Center remains a global centre of the arts, particularly following a recent $175-million expansion that added art installations, scenic walkways and gardens, more performing spaces and a huge outdoor video wall with terrace seating. A former warehouse district north of Massachusetts Ave has become a foodie magnet following the opening of Union Market, with its dozens of gourmet vendors. The neighbourhood, rechristened as NoMa, continues to earn fans, particularly with the arrival of La Cosecha, a sprawling Latin American food hall and marketplace that opened in 2019. These are fine additions to a city that's always had a lot going

The award-winning facade of the National Museum of African American History & Culture

© RARRARORRO | SHUTTERSTOCK

'One of my favorite spots is Compass Rose in DC's U Street Corridor. Compass Rose specialises in shared plates of international street foods – you can't go wrong, but my favourite is the Georgian khachapuri.'

-Greta Kaufman, Adams Morgan resident

for it – from fabulous free museums to leafy neighbourhoods that invite long days of urban exploring.

UNMISSABLE EXPERIENCES

The National Museum of African American History & Culture provides a moving portrait of the African American experience, from the horrors of slavery to the world-changing contributions of people of colour across countless fields, including music, literature, theatre, fine arts and sports. The architecturally striking building, conceived by David Adjure, features a crown-like stack of galleries covered in bronze plates, and it was named the Beazley Design of the Year in 2017. Inside, interactive state-of-the-art exhibits do a masterful job of bringing the past to life. Not surprisingly, this museum is extremely popular. Go online to reserve a timed entry pass before you arrive.

TIME YOUR VISIT

April to mid-June is Washington's peak season, when the weather is most pleasant, though hotel prices are highest. This is also when you'll find big events, such as the National Cherry Blossom Festival (late March to mid-April). Summers (late June to early September) are steamy in DC, and the winters (December to early March) bring regular snowstorms.

• By Regis St Louis

ITINERARY
Two days in Washington, DC

● Go for a walk (or a run!) along the **Washington Mall**. Don't miss the powerful Vietnam Veterans Memorial, the stately Lincoln Memorial and the inspiring Martin Luther King, Jr Memorial.

● Spend the afternoon taking in the trove of fabled artworks at the **National Gallery of Art**, one of DC's many celebrated (free!) museums.

● Ogle the produce and feast on fresh crab cakes at the photogenic **Eastern Market**, with a surrounding sea of arts and crafts vendors on weekends.

● Stroll the cobblestone streets of leafy **Georgetown**. Stop for coffee at Grace Street Coffee Roasters, grab lunch at venerable Martin's Tavern and admire the Potomac views at Georgetown Waterfront Park.

4 Georgetown

National Gallery of Art

1 Washington Mall

2

3 Eastern Market

CAIRO, EGYPT

Egypt waved Tutankhamun's treasures off on a globetrotting tour in 2018, declaring it the last time the pharaoh's burial-booty would leave its shores. Want to gawk at ancient Egypt's wealth in the future? You'll need to visit Cairo's Grand Egyptian Museum (GEM). The year 2020 is set to be the date – *inshallah* (God willing) – this state-of-the-art museum in Giza throws open its doors. Head here to marvel at a mind-boggling collection in what will be the world's largest museum entirely committed to one civilisation. For Red Sea and Luxor holidaymakers, a Pyramids and GEM add-on will also become a doddle with Giza's newly inaugurated Sphinx Airport set to operate domestic flights.

The endlessly mysterious Great Sphinx and Great Pyramid

© ANTON BELO / SHUTTERSTOCK

03

A shopfront on Sharia Al Muizz, one of the oldest streets in Cairo

© EFESENKO / SHUTTERSTOCK

Population: 22 million
Language: Arabic
Unit of currency: Egyptian pound
How to get there: Cairo Airport is Egypt's main air-hub with direct flights from cities in Europe, North America and Asia.

TELL ME MORE...

Cairo will slap your senses alive like few other cities can in a jubilant mash-up of furious noise and crowd-crush. The Pyramids sit out on the edge where Giza's slumping suburban sprawl gives way to the sand. Deep in the belly of the city, where the Nile snakes in languorous loops, Downtown thumps to a constant backbeat of bellowing car-horns. Here shisha cafes and street-food joints jostle for pavement space, loomed over by 19th-century facades slowly getting a facelift as their blackened top layers are scraped off. Further east, the past seeps through the pavement cracks of Islamic Cairo's wriggling alleys where the medieval city of Al-Qahira was born. Many of the mosques, madrassas and mausoleums here, including the venerated Al Azhar Mosque, have been finely

ITINERARY
Three days in Cairo

● Uncover **Downtown Cairo**'s street-food scene on a Bellies En-Route culinary tour led by Egyptian foodies.

● Soak up history inside the city's oldest synagogue, church and mosque then view dazzling Coptic art inside the **Coptic Museum**.

● Delve into the claustrophobic corridors of the **Great Pyramid**. Fingers crossed, the **Grand Egyptian Museum** will be open in Giza as well.

● Don't miss the **Museum of Islamic Art**, buying handmade textiles in the **Tentmakers Market** and standing amid Mamluk majesty inside the **Mosque-Madrassa of Sultan Hassan** in Cairo's medieval Islamic district.

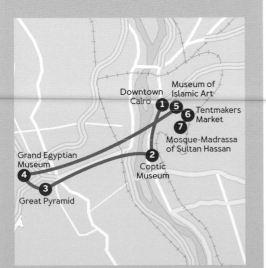

'For me Downtown Cairo is the living, breathing, pulsing, and sometimes screaming, heart of the city. It enlivens me, frustrates me but never bores me! Experience it!'
-Nigel Hetherington, archaeologist and founder of Past Preservers

restored in recent years. Cairo has always been rich pickings for history geeks. The GEM is simply the cherry on top.

UNMISSABLE EXPERIENCES

● Visit the Pyramids of Giza – the giant tombs of the fourth-dynasty pharaohs have been gobsmacking travellers since Herodotus wrote about them in the 4th century BC. By then they were already over 2000 years old.

● Look for locally made crafts in Khan Al Khalili, a medieval mall in business since the 14th century. Forgo the main drag's tourist-tat to fossick for Bedouin rag-rugs and metal lamps in the surrounding alley squiggles.

● On Wednesday nights head to Makan, a performance space dedicated to preserving Egypt's diverse folk-music traditions, to experience the haunting and trance-like *zar*, a female healing ritual.

TIME YOUR VISIT

October to April is prime visiting time. In 2020, Ramadan (the Muslim month of fasting) is estimated to fall between 24 April to 23 May. Although many visitors avoid Ramadan, during this month festivities take over Cairo's streets after dark so it can be fascinating fun for flexible travellers.

• By Jessica Lee

Al Azhar Mosque and university, founded in AD 970, is still Egypt's main centre of Islamic study

GALWAY, IRELAND

Brilliantly bohemian Galway is arguably Ireland's most engaging city. Here brightly painted pubs heave with live music; cafes offer front-row seats to watch buskers perform. And this year all that creative exuberance is being supercharged by events marking Galway's role as a 2020 European Capital of Culture – the city's calendar is as packed with activity as the bars are with locals on a Saturday night. Expect street spectacle, live and digital art as well as world-class music, theatre and dance. Sleep might have to wait – in Galway even the buskers play late into the night. Vivid and vibrant, brimful of imagination, Galway in 2020 is home to a year-long, city-wide, arty party. And you're invited too.

The city's colourful waterfront, beside Galway Bay

© SFABISUK / GETTY IMAGES

Population: 79,934

Languages: English, Irish

Unit of currency: Euro

How to get there: Hourly buses link Galway with its three closest airports: Shannon Airport and Knock Airport (both one hour's drive), and Ireland's main airport at Dublin (a 2½-hour drive).

TELL ME MORE...

Galway pulses with music. It pours from the pubs and flows through the streets. Everywhere you'll find impromptu jam sessions of fiddles, tin whistles and pipes. And in Galway it's utterly

'For me the real Galway is the people, the chats, the laughs and the "howya's". There's true rapport between chefs and local producers and great energy about our beers, whiskey, fish and fantastic dairy – Irish butter is the best thing going!'

-Sheena Dignam, tour guide & founder of Galway Food Tours

authentic; the music sessions delighting the tourists happen whether you're here or not. And it's not just music. Here galleries, theatres and bookshops sustain a tangible artistic tradition, a love of visual arts and words. Galwegians also make an art form of conversations. Pubs and cafes ripple with wit that's as rich as the pints of part-poured Guinness settling slowly before being topped up at the bar. Which makes ordering a drink, crowding into a music pub snug or ordering a meal a conversational delight. You get all this in any year. But this year, Capital of Culture events are amplifying the city's creative diary. In Ireland, *craic* means gossip, fun and good times. In Galway in 2020, prepare for some serious *craic*.

UNMISSABLE EXPERIENCES

● Live music sits at the centre of the city's soul, best experienced among the pints and bar stools at Tig Cóilí, where the walls are decorated with photos of those who've played

Galway is famous for its
fresh oysters

© MARIA KOVALEVA / SHUTTERSTOCK

ITINERARY
Two days in Galway

● **Eyre Square** sits in the centre, a
broad space studded with sculptures and
surrounded by pubs.
● Busker-dotted streets lead to
McCambridge's, a cafe and deli specialising in
local foods; there's a whiskey-tasting table too.
● From bar-lined Quay St, Druid Lane leads
to the **Hall of the Red Earl**, the striking ruins of a
13th-century banqueting house.
● Cross the swift-flowing River Corrib to the
West End, which for many locals is the 'real'
Galway. There the **Crane Bar** is a top spot for
traditional music and dancing.

there, and two live *céilidh* sessions a day draw
the crowds.
● Just chatting is a joy in Galway. At the Tigh
Neachtain pub, timber walls frame a roaring
fire and locals crack gentle jokes that spark
conversations and make you feel at home.
● Galway's culinary heart beats strongest at
Loam, where groundbreaking flavour combos
and home-grown, locally sourced and foraged
ingredients rule: expect dried hay, fresh moss,
wild oats and peat-smoked ice cream.

TIME YOUR VISIT
Finer weather and great events make spring
to autumn a tempting time. Top-name authors
arrive in April for the Cúirt International Festival;
early-July's Galway Film Fleadh features
edgy flicks. July also brings the prestigious
Galway International Arts Festival, while late-
September's Galway International Oyster and
Seafood Festival draws food-loving crowds.
• By Belinda Dixon

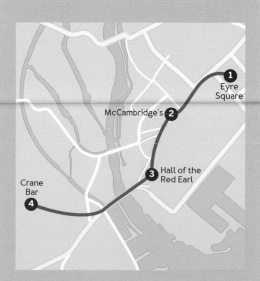

McCambridge's **2**

1
Eyre
Square

3 Hall of the
Red Earl

Crane
Bar
4

BONN, GERMÁNY

The old and new
towers of Bonn

▆▆▆▆ **Once capital of West Germany,** Bonn slipped off the radar when Berlin reseized the reins in 1990. But it's back in the spotlight with a cymbal roll in 2020, as the city gears up to mark Beethoven's 250th birthday. What's the score? Well, you can expect a year-round line-up of concerts drawing world-famous orchestras, soloists and conductors (among them Sir Simon Rattle and Daniel Barenboim). Beyond this, there are installations and competitions tuning into Beethoven's musical genius, picnic performances, and 'home concerts' where local musicians fling open their doors to the public. Theater Bonn is staging *Fidelio*, the composer's only opera, while the newly revamped Beethovenhalle, the city's premier concert hall, is set to reopen in time for the festivities.

© TRAVELVIEW / SHUTTERSTOCK

Population: 325,490

Language: German

Unit of currency: Euro

How to get there: Cologne Bonn Airport is 20km north of central Bonn and has flights to 130 cities across Europe. It's linked to the Hauptbahnhof by shuttle bus. Frequent trains link the city to major destinations across the country, such as Cologne, one hour away.

TELL ME MORE...

Bonn has often unjustly been brushed aside in favour of sexier cities, but as you wander the lanes of its medieval Altstadt to the whimsically spired minster and stately Hofgarten, you might just get an inkling of the romance that fired Beethoven's imagination. The Rhine flows as gently through Bonn's heart as the maestro's Ninth Symphony, and it is here that cafes, wine bars and beer gardens spring to life with the first tentative rays of sunshine. The culture-loaded sights of the Museumsmeile are several tram stops south.

Bonn might not have the hipster cachet of Berlin, say, but it reveals itself in a whole new edgy light in the formerly working-class Nordstadt, where a growing crop of boutiques, coffee roasteries, craft beer bars and new-wave galleries are indicative of a city that rightly has its mojo back as it swaggers into 2020.

UNMISSABLE EXPERIENCES

● Visit the Beethoven-Haus on Bonngasse, the humble home where the classical music colossus was born in 1770. Scores, instruments, letters, ear trumpets and his last grand piano give insight into his musical genius.

● Take a romp through post-WWII German history at the Haus der Geschichte on Bonn's culture-driven Museumsmeile. Star exhibits

ITINERARY
Three days in Bonn

● Kick off with a mosey around the lanes of the **Altstadt**, which spirals around the **Münsterplatz** and its slender-steepled Gothic minster. Romanesque origins survive in the cloister.

● Immerse yourself in the works of German expressionist painter **August Macke** (1887–1914) at the house where he lived in the three years before his untimely death on the battlefields of WWI.

● Glide along the River Rhine on a boat trip departing from **Brassertufer**. A popular day trip heads to the craggy, wooded, castle-encrusted **Siebengebirge**.

● When the sun's out, the huge, tree-canopied **Biergarten Alter Zoll** in the Stadtgarten is where it's at. Sip a cold foamy one as barges drift along the Rhine below.

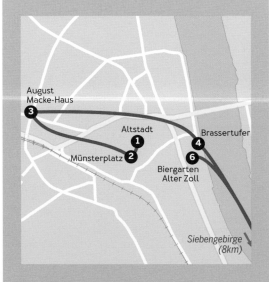

Castle Drachenburg sits atop a forested hill in Siebengebirge, a short boat journey from Bonn

© DIHETBO | SHUTTERSTOCK

'I love Bonn's unique flair and the fact that it's the birthplace of Beethoven. Here tradition and culture merge with modernity – in architecture as in music, with Beethoven's works constantly being staged in new, innovative ways.'

-Stefan Hartmann, *project manager of Beethoven Jubilee Year 2020*

include a *Rosinenbomber* (Candy Bomber) plane and cult VW campervans.

● Explore the architecturally innovative Kunstmuseum Bonn, and its prized collection of 20th-century art, with high-calibre works by August Macke and other Rhenish expressionists hanging alongside avant-gardists like Beuys and Baselitz.

TIME YOUR VISIT

Bonn is a riot of pink cherry blossom in spring (especially in Nordstadt). Musical headliners include the Jazzfest in May and the Beethovenfest in September. Summers are mild and made for idling, with Rhine cruises, beer-garden afternoons and open-air festivals.

• By Kerry Walker

TOP 10 CITIES

LA PAZ, BOLIVIA

Perhaps it's the Jetsonian capsules gliding over La Paz along the world's largest cable-car system that are the most obvious signs of its new-found ambition. There were just three lines in 2014, but there will be 11 in 2020. Down below, the once-drab city is racing towards a more radiant and inspired future. Everyone from a flamboyant self-taught architect to the budding chefs leaving new culinary schools is thriving here – not because of some borrowed ideas and global trends, but rather due to a renewed sense of pride in Bolivia's indigenous roots. To be unabashedly Bolivian in the Bolivian capital is, nearly 200 years after independence, finally a fashionable idea.

Calle Jaén,
La Paz's best-
preserved
colonial street

© JESS KRAFT / SHUTTERSTOCK

Handcrafted artefacts on display at Mercado de las Brujas

© SAIKO3P / SHUTTERSTOCK

Population: 2.3 million
Languages: Spanish, Aymara, Quechua
Unit of currency: Boliviano
How to get there: El Alto International Airport receives flights from major South American hubs. Buses link the city with destinations in northern Chile and southern Peru (including Cuzco).

TELL ME MORE...

Touching down at the world's highest international airport, it becomes immediately obvious that La Paz has some unique geography. Half of it (technically the separate city of El Alto) lies on the Altiplano above 4000m in altitude. There is much international buzz here about the works of Aymará architect Freddy Mamani, whose Technicolor New Andean style shocks the senses like an Ayahuasca fever dream.

The rest of the city lies down below in a deep earthen bowl. Spurred by the 2012 opening of Gustu (from New Nordic Cuisine founder Claus Meyer), chefs here are looking to their grandparents for inspiration in crafting a novel Bolivian cuisine based on 100% native products. Add in a clutch of new design hotels and concept stores and it's not hard to see why an increasing number of tourists are now sticking around in La Paz before they venture further afield.

UNMISSABLE EXPERIENCES

● From Andean grains to Amazonian fruits, taste the larder of Bolivia in one of the city's lauded new restaurants. Top choices include Popular Cocina Boliviana for lunch, Los Qñapés for an afternoon snack and high-end vegan restaurant Ali Pacha for dinner.
● Stock up on amulets, herbal viagras and other folk remedies at the so-called witches' market, Mercado de las Brujas. While there, get your fortune read in coca leaves by one of the wandering *yatiris* (traditional healers).

The Mi Teleférico cable car

© SAIKO3P / GETTY IMAGES

'There is a pride in serving our traditional foods and Bolivian products that you wouldn't have seen in La Paz five years ago.'

-Marsia Taha, head chef at Gustu

● Test fate on a day-long mountain-bike trip from the Altiplano down to the steamier climes of the Yungas forest along the so-called World's Most Dangerous Road, the North Yungas Road.

TIME YOUR VISIT

Temperatures don't vary all that much in La Paz, although it can dip below freezing in the winter months (June–September). Summer (December–March) is the wet season, which can make onward travel to the lowlands extremely difficult. The shoulder seasons in between offer pleasant weather and cheaper prices.

• By Mark Johanson

ITINERARY
One day in La Paz

● Witness 50 shades of neon on a tour of Freddy Mamani's New Andean architecture in **El Alto**.

● Ride the Mi Teleférico cable car down to the fashionable Zona Sur neighbourhood for lunch at **Gustu**.

● Head uptown to check the pulse of the nation at **Plaza San Francisco**, a famous square filled with artists, activists and *lustrabotas* (shoeshiners).

● Stroll over to the historic Casco Viejo neighbourhood to take some snaps in **Plaza Murillo**, educate yourself at the **Museo de Etnografía y Folklore** and wander down cobblestoned **Calle Jaén**.

● Cap the day off with a *singani* cocktail and Bolivian tapas at a local *peña* (folk music club) such as **Jallalla**.

6 Calle Jaén
7 Jallalla
5 Museo de Etnografía y Folklore
3 Plaza San Francisco
Gustu (10km);
El Alto (3km)
4 Plaza Murillo

KOCHI, INDIA

This nicely chilled city in southern India has seen the light. Grafted onto the tropical Malabar Coast in Kerala, Kochi has become a shining example in renewable energy in recent years, launching the world's first fully solar-powered airport, which snagged it a UN Champions of the Earth award. But that's just tip-of-the-iceberg stuff. With boho cafes, intimate homestays hidden away in lazy, colonial-era backstreets, and a raft of forward-thinking galleries, this city keeps a tight grip on its heritage while wholeheartedly embracing its newfound cool. In 2020, street art comes to the fore at Kochi-Muziris Biennale, putting India firmly on the contemporary arts festival map.

A classical
Kathakali
performance

Population: 2.1 million

Languages: Malayalam, English

Unit of currency: Indian rupee

How to get there: Kochi International Airport, the main point of arrival, is 30km north of mainland Ernakulam. Alternatively, you can reach Kochi by train from Trivandrum (4½ hours), Kerala's capital. Regular ferries connect Ernakulam and historic Fort Cochin.

'Kochi is my home town and for me it's the sea and the cultural influences of the French, Portuguese and British that make it so special. I can't travel the world, but by running a homestay the world comes to me. I welcome my guests like members of my own family.'

–Michael Vadakkevettil, owner, Michaela Homestay

TELL ME MORE...

India moves to a relaxed, liberal groove in Kochi. Born from the great flood of the River Periyar in 1341, the city has drawn spice traders, travellers and explorers for centuries to its European-flavoured streets, bearing the architectural imprint of the Dutch, Portuguese and British Raj. And the doors are still open, with some 200 homestays lodged in converted colonial villas that swing stylistically from intimate and old-fashioned to boutique-chic. Here the guesthouse-as-home concept comes into its own, with hosts providing lavish breakfasts, endless stories and Keralan cookery tips. Kochi is a cultural one-off, pivoting effortlessly between past and present, heritage and hipster, urban and outdoors. Here Christians, Jews, Hindus and Muslims live harmoniously side by

ITINERARY
Three days in Kochi

● Make the pilgrimage to India's oldest European church, **St Francis**, built in 1503, where intrepid Portuguese explorer Vasco da Gama was originally buried.

● Get the perfect shot of the giant **Chinese fishing nets** in action, then buy the day's catch at the fishmongers behind them (restaurants on **Tower Rd** will cook it for you).

● Jump in an auto rickshaw to Jew Town for a nose around 16th-century **Pardesi Synagogue**. India's oldest synagogue is ornately clad in hand-painted floor tiles, Belgian chandeliers and coloured lanterns.

● Catch a spine-tingling Kathakali theatre-dance performance at **Kerala Kathakali Centre**, a beautiful wood-lined theatre. Arrive before the show to see the elaborate make-up being applied to the performers.

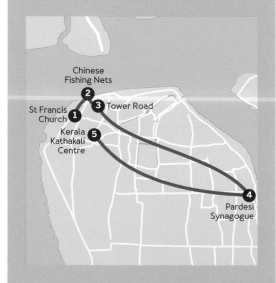

© ALEXANDER MAZURKEVICH / 500PX

Fort Kochi's photogenic
Chinese fishing nets

side. One minute you're touring India's oldest church, the next you're roaming the spice bazaars of synagogue-topped Mattancherry, or hiring a boat to paddle you into the mazy, lily-clogged backwaters as dusk falls and the evening puja (prayer) begins.

UNMISSABLE EXPERIENCES

● Watch teams of grizzled fishers operate Fort Kochi's giant cantilevered Chinese fishing nets to reel in the day's catch. These spider-like, bamboo-and-teak contraptions recall the legacy of traders from the AD 1400 court of Kublai Khan. Come at dusk to see and photograph them silhouetted against a peach-gold sky.

● Gawp at opulent Mattancherry Palace, a Portuguese gift to the Raja of Kochi in

1555, which was restored to its glory by the Dutch in 1663. The palace's pride and joy are its outstandingly preserved Hindu murals, recounting scenes from the Ramayana, Mahabharata and Puranic legends in intricate, colourful detail.

TIME YOUR VISIT

December to March is peak season, with warm days, cool nights, room rates at a premium and crowd-pulling events such as the Kochi-Muziris Biennale and costumed parades and elephants at Kochi Carnival. July to November brings monsoon rains and the occasional cyclone. Homestays are bargainous from April to June, when temperatures soar.

• By Kerry Walker

Exploring the Kochi
backwaters by boat

VANCOUVER, CANADA

████ This natural playground – squeezed **majestically** between the blue waters of the Pacific and the forest-clad mountaintops of the North Shore – was the birthplace of Greenpeace, so it seems fitting that the city has been trying to lead the world in urban sustainability. And for you, the environmental benefits of its longstanding Greenest City 2020 Action Plan will only enrich your stay. Take to its vastly expanded cycling and walking network, including an unforgettable 28km section along beaches and shorefront, and comfortably hop between the city's many sights on an upgraded public transport system. Or simply catch some shade under one of the 102,000 new trees that have been planted since 2010.

Population: 2.5 million
Language: English
Unit of currency: Canadian dollar
How to get there: Vancouver International Airport is Canada's second-busiest airport, with direct flights to much of North America, the Pacific Rim and Europe. The city is also served by both bus and rail, and is an easy hour's drive north of the US border.

'I'm continually drawn to the beauty and solitude that nature provides. So, for me, Vancouver is the perfect city. The immediate access to the outdoors and the temperate climate are also the perfect incubator for my kids to share in my passion.'
-Hamish Weatherly, Vancouver resident

TELL ME MORE...
Even within downtown's sea of gleaming skyscrapers, there always seems to be a tempting sightline to either the mountains or the ocean. Nature isn't something to visit outside Vancouver – it is an intrinsic part of the city itself. Locals, typically clad in either Gore-Tex or Lycra (depending on the season), embrace their stunning surrounds every chance they get – follow their lead. In summer you can swim, paddleboard or kayak off numerous beaches, cycle, walk or rollerblade around the justifiably glorified Stanley Park Seawall or hike up to the summit of Grouse Mountain (if you start early enough, you can hit a beach, the Seawall and Grouse in a single day). Come winter, the seashore still calls for a stroll or cycle, and the local mountains are carpeted in snow for skiing and boarding till 10pm. Yet, the metropolis has its pulls too, with some incredible museums,

Landmark Science World on the banks of False Creek

open-air markets, countless independent coffee houses and North America's best Asian cuisine.

UNMISSABLE EXPERIENCES
● Embracing the ocean, and encircling 400 hectares of parkland and rainforest, the Stanley Park Seawall offers walkers, runners, cyclists and rollerbladers constantly changing (but always spellbinding) views of mountains, city skylines and sea from its many twists and turns.
● Flanked by yachts, shaded by Granville Bridge and home to numerous art studios and boutique shops, Granville Island is the perfect spot for an afternoon picnic after exploring its bountiful public market.

©DAN BRECKWOLDT / SHUTTERSTOCK

ITINERARY
Two days in Vancouver

● If the sun is shining, head straight for the **Stanley Park Seawall**. Finish at English Bay Beach and savour a world-class cinnamon bun at **Delany's Coffee House**.

● Tour **False Creek** on a petite passenger ferry before disembarking at **Granville Island Public Market**.

● Shop your way west through the seaside neighbourhood of **Kitsilano**, then continue up the hill to the University of British Columbia for a visit to the heralded **Museum of Anthropology**.

● Make time to wander historic **Gastown** in the city centre, as well as the colourful corners of Chinatown nearby.

● Save an evening for dinner and drinks on **Commercial Drive**.

● For a Vancouver-style workout, hike 'the Grind' – nature's ultimate stair master – to scenic delights atop Grouse Mountain, or take the gondola up for some easy-access snow sports during winter.

TIME YOUR VISIT

With warm temperatures and dryish skies, June to September is best to explore the city, its forests and seashore. Winter is mild and rainy at sea level, but atop the North Shore mountains the precipitation falls as snow, which makes December to March ideal for skiing, boarding and snowshoeing.

• By Matt Phillips

Vancouver's favourite outdoor hangout, the Stanley Park Seawall

TOP 10 CITIES

DUBAI, UAE

The future is now in Dubai as the superlative-craving emirate launches several boundary-pushing marquee projects in 2020. Top billing, of course, goes to the six-month-long World Expo 2020, where 180 nations go all out in showcasing the latest visions in sustainability and mobility (think: flying cars) in architecturally showstopping pavilions. Also expected to open is the Museum of the Future, a cabinet of next-gen wonders in an eye-shaped building festooned with calligraphy. Meanwhile, two miles off-shore, a Europe-themed fantasy resort on an artificial archipelago called The World is gearing up to welcome its first guests to such only-in-Dubai phenomena as underwater bedrooms and year-round snow.

Burj Khalifa dwarfs the rest of Dubai

Population: 3.1 million

Languages: Arabic, English, Urdu

Unit of currency: Arab Emirate dirham

How to get there: Dubai International Airport is the main gateway and one of the world's busiest airports. The even bigger Al Maktoum International Airport is under construction near the World Expo grounds but thus far receives few commercial flights.

TELL ME MORE...

The most glamorous of the seven sheikhdoms that make up the United Arab Emirates, Dubai is famous for being a go-go society driven by the hunt for world records (tallest building, biggest mall, etc) and as a laboratory of out-there projects that elsewhere would never see the light of day (skiing in the desert, palm-shaped islands). The food is fabulous, the nightlife world class, the shopping unparalleled. And if you lift the cliché lid just a bit, you'll also stumble upon such street-cred gems as an urban-gritty gallery district, buzzy indie boutiques and bold street art. Never one to rest on its laurels, Dubai has been busy expanding its portfolio of attractions in the run-up to Expo 2020. Joining such iconic headliners as the Burj Khalifa and Dubai Mall are the giant Ain Dubai Ferris wheel, food-and-fun zones such as the beachfront La Mer and

The Jumeirah Mosque is one of only a handful in the UAE that is open to non-Muslims

© STEVE LOVEGROVE / SHUTTERSTOCK

ITINERARY
Two days in Dubai

● Get a primer on Islamic architecture and religion on a tour of the snow-white **Jumeirah Mosque**.

● Spread your towel on hip **Kite Beach** with its food trucks, plenty of sports action and free wifi.

● Watch the sun plunge into the Gulf behind the iconic Burj Arab, cocktail in hand, from the modern-Arabian village that is **Madinat Jumeirah**.

● Unleash your power shopper at the village-sized **Dubai Mall** without missing its three-story aquarium, giant dino, and dancing fountains.

● Ferret out authentic low-cost feasts from India to Iran in **Bur Dubai**'s expat kitchens or have the expert guides of Frying Pan Adventures take you there.

'The snack stalls of Meena Bazaar in Old Dubai come to life after the sun goes down and global treats like chaats, kulfi and mithai make for a fun culinary journey.'

-Abhiroop Sen, director of Communication Strategy

the Creekside Al Seef, the Al Shindagha Museum and the Jameel Arts Centre.

UNMISSABLE EXPERIENCES

● Conquer the Burj Khalifa, the world's reigning tallest building, which kisses the clouds at 828m and also lays claim to other world records, such as most floors, highest outdoor observation deck, highest restaurant and longest elevator.

● Soak up an *Arabian Nights* vibe in the Deira souqs: a maze of lanes where you can stock up on cardamom and saffron in the Spice Souq, shiny baubles in the Gold Souq and heady scents in the Perfume Souq.

● Connect with life in Dubai before the discovery of oil at the Dubai Museum, housed in the 1787 Al Fahidi Fort, or the brand-new Al Shindagha Museum.

TIME YOUR VISIT

World Expo 2020 runs from October 2020 until April 2021. During those months, temperatures hover around 30°C, although nights are cool and rain is a possibility. Between June and September, the heat and humidity will have you craving air-con most of the time. The approximate dates of Ramadan in 2020 are 24 April to 23 May.

• By Andrea Schulte-Peevers

10

DENVER, USA

Denver's elevated position as one of the USA's most charming boomtowns has reached new heights as the Mile High City enters its latest phase of growth, creative energy and damn good food. Construction cranes dot the mountain-studded horizon and empty lots turn into hip new hotels seemingly overnight, while new food halls such as Milk Market satisfy appetites with an eclectic mix of farm-to-table and international fare. In 2020, the mind-bending Santa Fe art experience Meow Wolf is set to come to Denver for a permanent $50-million installation, while the fascinating Kirkland Museum of Fine & Decorative Art has moved into a magnetic Olson Kundig–designed building within the city's Golden Triangle Creative District.

The Rocky Mountains loom over the Denver skyline

The 400ft sandstone rocks of the Red Rocks Amphitheatre create awesome acoustics for live concerts

© CAPTURE LIGHT | SHUTTERSTOCK

Population: 3.2 million

Language: English

Unit of currency: US dollar

How to get there: Denver International Airport is the largest airport in the USA by land area, with direct flights to major hubs in a variety of international destinations. A light-rail line shuttles passengers from the airport to the city centre. Amtrak's California Zephyr arrives daily from Chicago on its way to San Francisco.

TELL ME MORE...

In a city that's always been tied to a frontier spirit of individualism and perseverance, a new breed of community has helped shape a cityscape where you're as likely to see a pair of cowboy boots as a Tesla. Optimistically experimental outfits such as Comal Heritage Food Incubator,

'The RiNo Art District used to be a food desert, but now we have access to some of the finest restaurants in the region – like Safta, Hop Alley and Cart & Driver.'

-Tracy Weil, president & co-founder, RiNo Art District

which fuses immigrant job training with quality international food, are popping up in dynamic new developments in previously industrial parts of town. Elsewhere, cultural touchpoints include the Denver Art Museum, the Clyfford Still Museum and the Boettcher Concert Hall, and make Denver the place to experience the greats, while up-and-coming creative haven River North Art District (aka RiNo) features fledgling artists,

ITINERARY
Three days in Denver

● Meander around Denver's **Union Station**, a beautifully restored train station that now serves as the city's main transport hub and hip meet-up spot.

● Peruse the galleries and museums clustered within the Golden Triangle Creative District. A great place to start is the **History Colorado Center**, which details the Centennial State's pioneer roots.

● Hop on a B-Cycle and try to keep up with the city's characteristically fit denizens along the **Cherry Creek Bike Path**.

● Sample flavours from around the world at **Zeppelin Station**, one of the city's newest food halls, which serves up such superb international fare as Vietnamese banh mi, Italian gelato, Nordic beef tartare and Hawaiian-style poke.

microbreweries and humming restaurants. Plus, two new hotels, the Ramble and the Source, have just opened in the heart of RiNo, making this neighborhood a perfect home base for exploring. With a well-established bike share, plus 137km of paved trails and an extensive public transport system, the city is easier to get around without a car than ever before.

UNMISSABLE EXPERIENCES

● Admire the art and architecture of the Denver Art Museum, which houses one of the country's largest collections of Native American art.

● Catch a show at Red Rocks Amphitheatre, a 9000-seat concert venue set between 120m-high red sandstone rocks. The naturally occurring amphitheatre has been the dramatic backdrop of live recordings of acts including U2, Neil Young and Phish.

● Savour the craft-beer scene at breweries such as Great Divide Brewing Co, which has won awards for its brews, such as the Yeti Imperial Stout, which has notes of caramel and toffee.

TIME YOUR VISIT

Denver receives around 300 sunny days a year. April to May and September to October feature shoulder-season prices and cooler temperatures. Summer is undoubtedly Denver's high season, as the city celebrates festivals such as the Juneteenth Music Festival and the Underground Music Showcase. During winter, the city's slope-loving residents fan out into the nearby Rocky Mountains, and great accommodation deals can be found all over the city.

• By Alexander Howard

LONELY PLANET'S

BEST VALUE
DESTINATIONS

East Nusa Tenggara, Indonesia / Budapest, Hungary
Madhya Pradesh, India / Buffalo, USA / Azerbaijan / Serbia / Tunisia
Cape Winelands, South Africa / Athens, Greece / Zanzibar, Tanzania

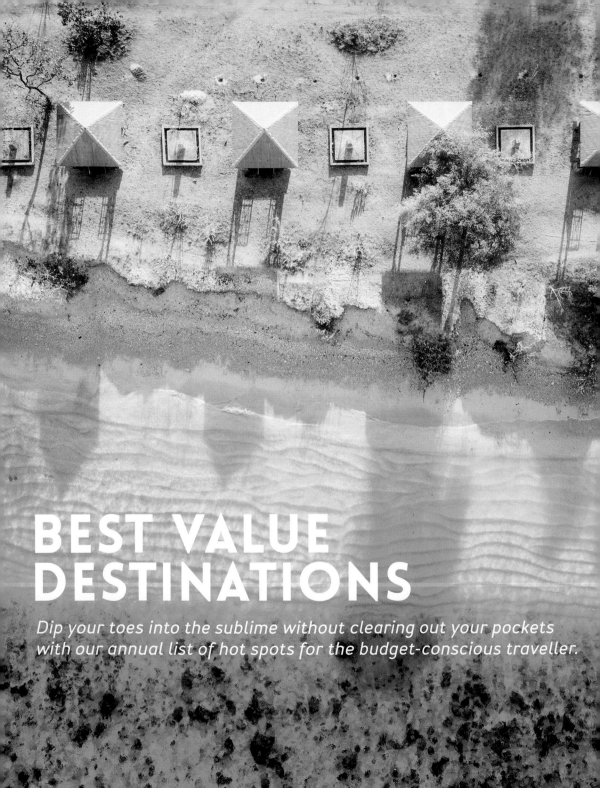

BEST VALUE
DESTINATIONS

Dip your toes into the sublime without clearing out your pockets with our annual list of hot spots for the budget-conscious traveller.

← 1 EAST NUSA TENGGARA, INDONESIA

This often-overlooked region of Indonesia rewards those who hit Bali and keep going – and going. These islands are home to pristine beaches that are quieter than those further west, and one of Indonesia's best diving scenes can be found on the Alor Archipelago. In places you'll still feel like a pioneer, and you'll certainly notice fewer crowds than on Bali, Lombok and the Gili Islands. With Komodo Island set to be closed in 2020 to allow the eponymous dragon population to recover, visitors should head to Rinca for their big-lizard fix. Wherever you go, the lower-key scene and reliance on independent travel will mean you're spending less money.

Basic boat trips are a popular way to travel between Lombok and Flores. This classic backpacker experience is a great way to see the country. Sleeping on deck keeps the cost lower still – but check what's included in the price.

↓ 2 BUDAPEST, HUNGARY

Of all the grand dames of Central Europe, Budapest is one of the most rewarding on your pocket, while serving up highlights memorable enough to rank high on continental explorers' lists of big-hitters. Aim for a less-visited thermal bath, where for a few dollars you get to wallow in the warm waters the city is famous for. Throughout the city you'll find buzzing wine bars, edgier 'ruin bars' in atmospheric old buildings and mod takes on the city's renowned cafe culture. Strolling the city's many art nouveau wonders, including Keleti station (still the best place to arrive in or depart Budapest), won't cost anything and will fill up your phone for happy Instagramming long after your trip comes to an end.

Many of the city baths have cheaper half-day or evening sessions which can cost considerably less than the full day entry. Don't forget your own swim cap and towel.

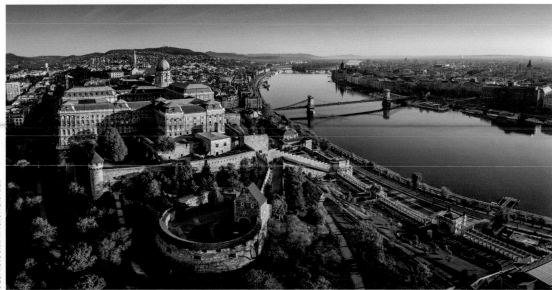

↓ 3 MADHYA PRADESH, INDIA

There's wildlife spotting with a difference in this state of India. The first difference is the price – wildlife-spotting excursions come with a far lower cost than in Africa. In the state's wildlife reserves, including Bandhavgarh Tiger Reserve and Pench National Park, there's lots to see beyond tigers; you might spy wild boar, spotted deer and langur monkeys. It's a slightly different experience to an African safari – tiger spotting is all about the mystery; the rare flashes of famous stripes through the forest, and it's not unusual to see nothing at all of the biggest of big cats. But your chances are getting better as numbers slowly recover. Elsewhere in the state you'll find celebrated sights such as Khajuraho's temples and the historic small towns of Orchha and Mandu that attract fewer visitors than big-name destinations in neighbouring Rajasthan. *Gwalior's fort and palaces make for a more laid-back stop after Agra, two hours down the track, and the city offers lower prices for almost everything in comparison.*

↑ 4 BUFFALO, USA

Buffalo's resurgence continues. Plan a visit now to take advantage of expanding budget air routes and a fast-growing hotel and restaurant scene. The city's super-interactive Children's Museum is new for 2020, and the recently restored Frank Lloyd Wright houses of the Graycliff Estate and Martin House Complex are another highlight. Visitors can explore the city's culinary scene at EXPO Market, a modern food hall, or take a tasting flight at Resurgence Brewing Company, a craft brewery in a former engine factory. Niagara Falls' tumbling water is an hour away by train or bus and makes a great day trip, with the added bonus of keeping you in Buffalo's more characterful accommodation choices.

Buffalo's vast City Hall is an art deco treasure. Explore it via a free tour starting at noon on weekdays and get a peek from the open-air observation deck.

© ALEXANDER MELNIKOV / 500PX

↑ 5 AZERBAIJAN

Azerbaijan is a near-unique destination with a low visiting cost for the quality of accommodation, food and experiences on offer. Baku, with its Caspian Sea waterfront, is home to ambitious architecture, fresh museums and a cosmopolitan air, energised by a growing global profile. Yes, you are still in Europe, even if once outside of Baku's Unesco-listed heart you're close to a mysterious landscape of mud volcanoes and burning earth. Visitors can then travel on into a hinterland of fast-changing towns and lost-in-time villages. The north and west of the country have the ever-present Caucasus as a backdrop, far from any crowds of visitors but always close to some of the most hospitable welcomes on offer anywhere.

Flights and accommodation in Baku are going to be the big financial outlays of a visit to Azerbaijan. Have a look at flight links through Budapest (Wizz Air) and Istanbul (Buta Airways) as a way to cut down on cost.

↗ 6 SERBIA

What's this? An authentic, characterful European country, rewarding slow exploration and barely discovered by travellers? Serbia can't even be said to have been hiding away – its capital, Belgrade, has for centuries been one of the continent's great crossroads. Today the city has laid-back cafe culture by day and budget-friendly partying by the Danube by night. And once you get out of Belgrade you'll have most of the country's delights to yourself. Outdoor adventures, spas and wineries, ancient monasteries and monolithic memorials from the Yugoslav era await.

Inexpensive bus links from Novi Sad come in handy if you're looking to extensively explore the villages and monasteries of the Fruška Gora National Park.

7 TUNISIA

Tunisia is a wonderful place to first dip your toes into North Africa at a reasonable cost. While Morocco offers a similar instant immersion, Tunisia's efforts to win back visitors means that it offers terrific value and also shines a light on what makes the country unique. Tunis' Medina, the remains of ancient Carthage and the beachside suburb of Sidi Bou Said offer a cultural counterpart to the country's seemingly endless range of beach options. Then there are things you can't find anywhere else – the easily accessible Saharan dunes, where Luke Skywalker first stared at twin suns, and the country's traditional Dar guesthouses, offering colourful and characterful accommodation.

Tunisia's (gender segregated) hammams offer a cheaper and more authentic steam and scrub than pricey equivalents in international hotels. Many of the most historic hammams are in Tunis, but local recommendation is the best guide.

↓ 8 CAPE WINELANDS, SOUTH AFRICA

South Africa is a regular fixture in lists of places that offer a friendly exchange rate for those looking for world-class safaris and other wildlife spotting, but there's much more to the country than Kruger and other reserves. A short journey from the fabulous food city of Cape Town is the country's wine region, centred on the historic towns of Franschhoek and Stellenbosch. The real action here is at the wineries and fabulous restaurants dotting the beautiful upland scenery. You won't find elephants snuffling round the vineyards, but you will find inexpensive tasting tours followed by lazy lunches serving world-class food alongside delicious local wines. If you care to stretch your wallet a little further when staying the night you can sleep it all off in high-end guesthouses and B&Bs that would cost a lot more elsewhere.

If you're planning on having a glass or two, a driver for a day, or longer, is easy to arrange. Cape Town airport is also easily accessed from the Winelands.

↓ 9 ATHENS, GREECE

The best things in Athens are free. Yes, the simply wondrous Acropolis Museum charges a modest fee, but you can gawp at the Parthenon itself from various vantage points for nothing. In fact, admiring the glowing Acropolis at night is one of the most magical experiences in Europe, let alone Greece. Athens beyond the Parthenon is a vast outdoor museum. You'll stumble over Byzantine churches and neoclassical buildings, including the National Library and University of Athens.

The city's pedestrianised centre makes for a more relaxed atmosphere than is often anticipated, and eating out is inexpensive. Beaches just outside the city, and day trips to the Temple of Poseidon at the end of Cape Sounion and the island of Aegina offer a quick and easy taste of the wonders of the rest of Greece.

Pack your sports gear for a morning run (access for runners: 7.30–9am) around the Panathenaic Stadium, setting for the 1896 Olympics.

BEST VALUE

BEST IN TRAVEL 2020

© EXPLORER | SHUTTERSTOCK

↗ 10 ZANZIBAR, TANZANIA

Such is the evocative nature of the word 'Zanzibar' that there's anticipation of adventure before you've even landed. And if arriving on the ferry from mainland Tanzania, you'll get an unusual internal passport stamp: bonus! Two passport stamps for the price of one. In Stone Town, stroll the ancient alleyways and enjoy magical sunsets before taking advantage of the cheap eats at the evening food market or its multicultural cafes. You'll delight in how much freshly grilled fare you can eat for so little. On the island's north and west coasts you can sample beach-side accommodation of all kinds at a price that will seem scarcely credible if you've tried to do the same in the Caribbean or Pacific Islands.

Though development has been fierce in the past 15 years, there are still quiet budget spots to hang your hammock in Nungwi, Bwejuu and Paje. If you want to stretch your budget further, aim to rest your head a block or two back from the beach.

• By Tom Hall

© AFRICANWAY | GETTY IMAGES

LONELY PLANET'S

THE
TRAVEL
EDIT

Best new openings / Best new places to stay
Best new food experiences / Best sustainable trips for families

BEST NEW OPENINGS

In 2020 there's a lot of new openings for travel nuts to get excited about. Some of these projects have been in the works for years and avid travellers should plan their holiday quickly in order to be among the first through the doors.

↑ 1 GRAND EGYPTIAN MUSEUM, GIZA, EGYPT

After years in the making, the ultimate museum for Egyptian history and treasure will finally open its doors to the public. A partial opening in 2020 is set to display all 5400 objects from Tutankhamun's tomb for the first time, exploring the king's history in meticulous detail. The collection also includes the 3200-year-old statue of Ramses II (above) and 20,000 previously unseen artefacts, to be displayed in galleries built more than 20m tall to accommodate them. This promises to be history on a truly grand scale. ***Begin to uncover the ancient mysteries in early 2020.***

2 GAME OF THRONES STUDIO TOUR, COUNTY DOWN, NORTHERN IRELAND

The HBO TV series may be over, but Westeros will live forever in the form of a permanent studio tour, with fully dressed sets, props and costumes immersing fans in Winterfell, Dragonstone, King's Landing and the lands beyond. There will also be a significant 'behind the scenes' element, showcasing craftwork from the armoury, costuming, art and make-up departments. The studio tour is the first in the *Game of Thrones* legacy projects, so you won't need to say goodbye to the Seven Kingdoms just yet.

The Westerosi winter returns in spring 2020.

3 QIANLONG GARDEN, FORBIDDEN CITY, BEIJING, CHINA

To mark the 600th anniversary of the Forbidden City, visitors will have access to the stunning Qianlong Garden for the first time. Spread across almost a hectare, it has four courtyards and 27 individual structures, all filled with exquisite interiors almost totally unchanged since the Imperial China period. A new visitor centre will be the gateway to this long-hidden treasure, which was originally built as a secret retirement hideaway for the fourth emperor of the Qing Dynasty and is now being lovingly restored.

The opening is part of the year-long anniversary celebrations in 2020.

4 DAWN CAFE, TOKYO, JAPAN

Robots are playing an increasingly visible role in the travel industry but – in this cafe at least – that doesn't mean faceless automation. Instead, the cyber-servers are controlled by people with severe mobility impairments who can use eye movements to get the robot to move around, take orders and even speak to customers. A pop-up trial in late 2018 was deemed a success and now a permanent base is in the works, opening up new employment opportunities for people to work from home or hospital.

Dawn Cafe is planned to be up and running before the 2020 Summer Olympics and Paralympics in July.

5 GRAB BICYCLE PATH, ROME, ITALY

At 45km, this promises to be the longest urban bike path in the world, running in a ring around Rome. Public works in Italy can be notoriously slow but, after years in development and gradual opening up of partial routes, 2020 might be the year you can finally feel the wind in your hair during a leisurely cycle around the Eternal City, taking in sights such as the Colosseum, St Peter's Basilica and the Appian Way.

The full cycle lane is planned for a 2020 opening.

6 THE EMBRACE, BOSTON, USA

This beautiful sculpture will be cast in bronze and is a fitting memorial for two of the greatest US citizens of all time: Martin Luther King, Jr and Coretta Scott King. It aims to inspire love and compassion in the community, calling to mind images of the couple embracing and walking arm-in-arm in protests. It will sit on the Boston Common, the finishing point of a 1965 march against segregation led by the civil rights icon. A King Center for Economic Justice to promote economic mobility in the Roxbury neighbourhood will also be established.

The tribute will be unveiled to the public in 2020.

© GREAT SOUTHERN

7 HYPERLOOP, DUBAI, UAE

The Hyperloop has been touted for a while as an ultra-speedy solution to crossing long distances at top speeds but so far has failed to materialise, despite hundreds of headlines. Now the theory looks to be finally put into practice and where better than the futuristic Dubai to test it out? While it won't connect to Abu Dhabi as promised anytime soon, the first 10km track is the public's first chance to test out the new mode of transport that might just revolutionise travel as we know it.

The Hyperloop is set to be part of the Dubai World Expo in October 2020.

↑ 8 GREAT SOUTHERN TRAIN JOURNEY, ADELAIDE– BRISBANE, AUSTRALIA

One of the latest luxury routes that prove rail travel will never die as long as people enjoy a day's leisurely journey through beautiful landscapes and a night of being gently rocked to sleep in their own private carriage, the Great Southern will run three- and four-day routes between Adelaide and Brisbane, offering opportunities to stop at national parks, beaches and cities, with a luxurious cabin and gourmet food options to enjoy onboard.

The inaugural season runs between 6 December 2019 and 27 January 2020.

9 CHINESE AMERICAN MUSEUM, WASHINGTON, DC, USA

The Chinese American experience will now have its own permanent museum in the US capital, telling stories of resilience and ingenuity stretching back more than 200 years. The exhibits and events will examine the early history of Chinese immigration in the USA, the unique merging of American and Chinese traditions and the evolution of contemporary Chinese American culture. The permanent exhibits are expected to have many artefacts donated by the public.

The museum will open in phases, starting in late 2019 and stretching out to 2020.

↓ 10 BLACKADORE CAYE, BELIZE

Leonardo DiCaprio bought this 42-hectare island back in 2005 with plans to transform it into an eco-resort that combines high sustainability with exclusive luxury. As well as being fully powered by renewable energy, it also promises to stop the island's trend of deforestation and overfishing. Half the island is earmarked for a wildlife reserve and research station, while there will be just 72 private accommodation suites elsewhere, along with strict eco-friendly rules about what can be brought onto the island.

The exclusive resort is predicting a 2020 opening.

• By AnneMarie McCarthy

BEST NEW PLACES TO STAY

From a boho option in Bora Bora to recycled bridge-keeper houses in Amsterdam and from a mountain lodge in Tennessee to a cattle station in northern Queensland, the year 2020 mixes sustainability with cutting-edge design.

© LEKKERWATER BEACH

↑ 1 LEKKERWATER BEACH LODGE, SOUTH AFRICA

While mountain zebras and giant antelopes wander the stunning fynbos-covered hills of the De Hoop Nature Reserve, it's the wonders offshore that make this new lodge so appealing. Its seven freestanding rooms, with floor-to-ceiling windows, are located along 6km of private beach and offer front-row seats to some of the world's best land-based whale watching.
From July to late November the waters off the reserve become filled with migrating southern right whales. www.naturalselection.travel

↗ 2 CANNÚA, COLOMBIA

Set into a steep slope within 11 hectares of protected Colombian forest is this new 18-room ecolodge. With complete sustainability as a goal, Cannúa is constructed from local bamboo and handmade compressed earth bricks. Guests can sit back and soak up the views of the valley below and the fragrances from the flower-filled garden, or strike out on indigenous trails from centuries past.
Cannúa is just 20 minutes' drive from the town of Marinilla and 45 minutes from José María Córdova International Airport. www.cannua.com

BEST NEW PLACES TO STAY

THE
TRAVEL
EDIT

BEST IN
TRAVEL
2020

© CANNUA

3 JUNGLE BAY, DOMINICA

Rebuilt following the devastating hurricanes of 2017, Jungle Bay overlooks the marine sanctuary of Scotts Head and Soufriere. The property has been guided by the principles set by the International Ecotourism Society and National Geographic's Center for Sustainable Destinations. Involvement with the local community is a founding principle, as are environmental conservation and construction of its eco-villas using sustainable resources. *Dominica's capital of Roseau is only a 20-minute drive away, while Douglas Charles Airport is 80 or so minutes away by road. www.junglebaydominica.com*

5 BLACKBERRY MOUNTAIN, USA

From the family behind the famed Blackberry Farm, this remarkable option resides on 2100 hectares of private parkland within the Great Smoky Mountains of Tennessee. Aimed to be both immersive and transformative, it offers guests the chance to embrace its pristine environment with scenic settings for meditation, mountain biking, bouldering, hiking and yoga. As they say, 'One mountain, many paths'. *Knoxville's McGhee Tyson Airport, which is linked to 25 other cities, is about half an hour's drive north. www.blackberrymountain.com*

5 MOUNT MULLIGAN LODGE, AUSTRALIA

Embrace the Australian outback and Mt Mulligan (Ngarrabullgan), an 18km-long flat-topped monolith, at this lodge in the northern reaches of Queensland. Built on a working cattle station by the Morris family, Mount Mulligan Lodge has used the United Nations Sustainable Development Goals as a framework and also endeavours to protect and restore the surrounding environment. *The rates for the four pavilions include all meals, Australian wines and beers, daily activities and use of a personal ATV. www.mountmulligan.com*

↑ 6 SWEETS HOTEL, THE NETHERLANDS

Breathing new life into 28 old bridge-operator cabins, some of which date back to the 17th century, the Sweets Hotel offers a truly novel way to experience Amsterdam. While there are no hotel-like services (think Airbnb apartment), these independent suites – each unique in design, furnishings and layout – are all found in scenic, watery locales throughout the captivating Dutch city.

All 28 cabins are one-bedroom suites designed for a maximum of two guests. No guests under the age of 21 are permitted. www.sweetshotel.amsterdam

7 ACE KYOTO, JAPAN

A short stroll from Nijō Castle, Museum of Kyoto, Kyoto Art Center and Nishiki Market, Ace Kyoto has been designed by Japanese architect Kengo Kuma, the man responsible for the new V&A Dundee in Scotland, The Opposite House hotel in Beijing and Tokyo's 2020 Olympic stadium. Laced with light and natural materials, the hotel revolves around open areas to generate both interaction and comfort. *The cherry-blossom (late March to early April) and autumn foliage (November) periods are inspiring times to visit. The quieter months of May and October are also rewarding. www.acehotel.com*

8 KEX PORTLAND, USA

Reykjavík hostel Kex made its name for its compelling interior and social spaces hewn from an old biscuit factory and decorated with salvaged industrial materials (reusing is more efficient than recycling). The group behind that gem have made an equally inspired transformation to the historic Vivian Apartments in Portland, Oregon. The hostel hosts a gastropub, live music venue, kitchen and sauna. *Kex Portland is located in the Central Eastside neighbourhood near the Burnside Bridge. The airport is 19km northeast of the city centre. www. kexportland.com*

⬈ 9 SOUL & SURF, PORTUGAL

The latest brainchild of surfing veterans Sofie and Ed Templeton, Soul & Surf in the Algarve aims to unite guests in an all-together, chilled way. Create bonds while being taught how to ride perfect waves, practising yoga under the sun or when dining communally on incredibly healthy fare. As a bonus, a percentage of its gross income supports a global environmental charity.

© SOUL & SURF, PORTUGAL

The chic farmhouse base of Soul & Surf is less than an hour's drive from Faro International Airport via the A22 toll road. www.soulandsurf.com

10 COQUI COQUI BORA BORA, FRENCH POLYNESIA

Matira Beach is the sublime setting for Coqui Coqui Bora Bora, the newest boho hotel offering from perfumer Francesca Bonato and her husband Nicolas Malleville. An exercise in understated elegance, each of the rattan-and-wood lined rooms are filled with flowing fabrics, fresh air and light. It's a refreshing step back onto shore from the many stilted options built directly over the waters elsewhere on the island. *If possible, try to coordinate your trip with the Heiva i Bora Bora in July or the Hawaiki Nui canoe race in November. www.coquicoqui.com/borabora*

• By Matt Phillips

BEST NEW FOOD EXPERIENCES

Globetrotting gourmands can't resist eating their way around the world (and documenting every spoonful) but in 2020 it's about a more mindful approach. Whether that translates as more diverse experiences, respecting the environment, questioning provenance or deliberately seeking out the female chefs, here are our ten suggestions for broadening your food-travel horizons.

→ 1 ALPINN, SOUTH TYROL, ITALY

The ideal setting for three-Michelin-starred chef Norbert Niederkofler's 'cook the mountain' philosophy, AlpiNN restaurant is perched at an altitude of 2275m on Mt Plan de Corones, overlooking the Dolomites and housed in the Lumen Museum of Mountain Photography. Open since December 2018, it uses only produce sourced from the region and has a relaxed ambience enjoyed by skiers, hikers and destination diners.
Choose from à la carte dining or set menus: two-course set menus start from €48. See www.alpinn.it/en for more details.

2 ALCHEMIST 2.0, COPENHAGEN, DENMARK

Fancy 50 courses over six hours? Since the spring of 2019, Alchemist 2.0 has been outshining its predecessor (which opened in 2015) in an extraordinary reincarnation. Chef Rasmus Munk presents his 'holistic cuisine' in a 20-times-bigger

in the Bay Area since it opened in May 2019. Inspired by the street food of Lagos, Nigeria, Simileoluwa is keen to demystify the culture's popular dishes, such as goat meat pepper soup, jollof spaghetti and moin moin.

Eko Kitchen is located at Joint Venture Kitchen, 167 11th St, and is open Friday to Sunday; see www.ekokitchensf.wixsite.com/nomnom for details.

4 L28 CULINARY PLATFORM, TEL AVIV, ISRAEL

This unique fine-dining restaurant run by NGO Start-Up Nation Central is also a chef accelerator: since October 2018, talented emerging Israeli chefs take six-month residencies here with culinary mentors. Shuli Wimer pioneered her mix of Israeli Galilee and Italian dishes here and handed the baton to Gabriel Israel and his North African-Ashkenazi menu in May 2019.

Lilienblum 28, Tel Aviv; check www.l28.co.il for current residencies; email reservations@l28-rest. com to book a table.

5 TASTE THE ISLAND FESTIVAL, IRELAND

This two-month festival debuted in mid-September 2019 and showcases some of the lesser-known Irish food and drink regions to the world, acknowledging travellers who want to enjoy authentic culinary experiences. Take a food trail; forage with experts; visit niche producers, distillers and brewers; partake in traditional skills. Oh and eat very well, in either small-town cafes or Michelin-starred establishments.

For more details on the festival program, see www.failteireland.ie.

(2230 sq metres) location in the former Danish Royal Theatre, which includes two sensory-experience rooms with actors, artists and installations presenting themes such as NYC and LGBTQ.

The new Alchemist is in Copenhagen's artsy Refshalevej neighbourhood and the set menu is around US$650. Book ahead at www.restaurant-alchemist.dk.

↑ 3 EKO KITCHEN, SAN FRANCISCO, USA

San Francisco's first Nigerian restaurant from financial analyst turned pop-up chef Simileoluwa Adebajo has been blazing a trail for African food

© ASHKAN MORTEZAPOUR PHOTOGRAPHY / SUPER LYAN

← 7 SUPER LYAN, AMSTERDAM, THE NETHERLANDS

Amsterdam's first on-tap cocktails come courtesy of the two-time World's Best Bar winner. Ryan Chetiyawardana (aka London's Mr Lyan) opened his first international outpost in April 2019. Expect his sustainability-meets-innovation approach and homemade stroopwaffles, bitterballen and vegan doughnuts in a stunning space with a 'traditional Dutch brown cafe' ethos, including a resident cat. *www.superlyan.com; Nieuwezijds Voorburgwal 3; it's open daily from 7am till late.*

8 DI STASIO CITTÀ, MELBOURNE, AUSTRALIA

Open since February 2019, this long-awaited venue from an Australian restaurant stalwart has more than met the sentimental hype. 'Ronnie' Di Stasio pioneered his first restaurant, Rosati, thirty years ago and now he's back in a beautiful Brutalist building, with video installations by Australian artists and the city's best pasta. *www.distasio.com.au/citta; 45 Spring St; open seven days from 11.30am till late.*

→ 9 KJOLLE, LIMA, PERU

Pia León's restaurant has had much fanfare since it opened in August 2018. The focus here is 100% Peruvian: the ingredients, the wood and stone used in the decor, and the Amazon-sourced cedar and capirona dishware. Pia was named by the World's 50 Best Restaurants as Latin America's Best Female Chef (2018). Then Kjolle (pronounced 'koy-ay') was shortlisted by the World Restaurant Awards for Arrival of the Year in 2019. She's cooked alongside her husband Virgilio Martínez for more than a decade. Now's her time! *www.kjolle.com; Av Pedro de Osma 301, Barranco; choose from the seven-course or à la carte menu.*

6 MERCADO LITTLE SPAIN, NYC, USA

An ambitious food hall from the famous Adrià brothers and Michelin-starred Spanish-American chef José Andrés opened in March 2019, bringing a touch of Spain's markets to the far west side of Manhattan but with a modern twist. Dine fast or slow: indulge in patatas bravas, churros or Galician empanadas, even pick up some Bomba rice to make your own authentic paella at home. *Visit www.littlespain.com for a preview of the 15 restaurants; take the No 7 subway from Times Square to Hudson Yards.*

BEST NEW FOOD EXPERIENCES

THE TRAVEL
EDIT

BEST IN
TRAVEL
2020

10 LA DAME DE PIC, SINGAPORE

The almost two-year restoration of Singapore's historic Raffles Hotel has rewarded patient food lovers in particular. Open since August 2019, the hotel houses not just new restaurants by Alain Ducasse and Jereme Leung but the Asian debut of three-Michelin-starred Anne-Sophie Pic. La Dame de Pic showcases her contemporary French cuisine interwoven with Singaporean flavours. *www.raffles.com/singapore/dining/la-dame-de-pic; book well in advance on +65 6337 1886 or singapore@raffles.com.*

• By Karyn Noble

BEST SUSTAINABLE TRIPS FOR FAMILIES

If your family loves to travel but you all worry about the environmental, social and economic effect of doing so, then it's time to take a more sustainable approach to your trips. We've identified ten destinations where you can minimise the impact of your family's travels.

1 AUSTRIA

Explore the kid-friendly Austrian capital of Vienna, which offers more organic farmland than any other city and has both 'Green Taxis' and plenty of bike-share stations for getting around. Find a small-scale farmstay for accommodation, then keep the family's legs moving by cycling, hiking and swimming in Weissensee. Make time for a visit to Werfenweng: a car-free, playground-rich lakeside town with green vehicles for visitors.

Vienna has a large number of playgrounds, some fantastic museums for children and the splendid Schloss Schönbrunn where kids can dress up.

BEST SUSTAINABLE TRIPS FOR FAMILIES

THE
TRAVEL
EDIT

BEST IN
TRAVEL
2O2O

↙ 2 FIJI

Leave the resorts and cruise ships behind and head off the beaten track to stay in a village homestay. Your kids will kids learn all about Fijian culture and your money will go directly to the community you're staying in. With older children you can go further and volunteer in both marine conservation and community projects, with the help of a reputable organisation.

If you do opt for a resort, stay at one such as Jean-Michel Cousteau Resort where guests can get involved in coral planting.

↑ 3 SAN FRANCISCO, USA

San Francisco is perfect for a break that will delight both the kids and satisfy your sustainability principles. The city banned plastic bags and bottles years ago, diverts 80% of its waste from landfill and has more than 1000 eco-friendly hotels. Plus most of the fun things to do with kids can be accessed without using a car and many involve green spaces, having fun on different forms of public transport and learning about sustainability.

Head to the Exploratorium: an incredible hands-on science museum in a purpose-built solar-powered building, which is aiming for zero net energy.

4 VOLCÁN TENORIO AREA, COSTA RICA

When you think about taking your kids to Costa Rica, you normally focus on viewing its incredible wildlife. But what about giving back to the human residents too? One way to support local communities and understand the Tico culture is by staying on a farm, and there are loads of lovely options around Volcán Tenorio and Río Celeste. Kids can take a hand in looking after animals and learning about traditional farming methods.

Base yourselves in Bijagua, a small town that's a big leader in rural community tourism due to the co-operative behind the Heliconias Rainforest Lodge.

5 WALES

For a relatively small area Wales packs a large punch in terms of sustainable activities for kids. Camp in one of many green campsites around Pembrokeshire or travel north to the Centre for Alternative Technology in Powys, where children can have fun learning about sustainable living. Don't forget to factor in a spin on the world's only people-powered rollercoaster at the eco-friendly Greenwood Forest Park in Snowdonia.

Find an environmentally friendly campsite in Wales here: www.greenercamping.org.

↓ 6 SOUTH AFRICA

As a country which has long had a responsible tourism policy, South Africa presents plenty of opportunities to explore its incredible culture and environment in a sustainable manner. It's also really fun for families, with easy wildlife viewing (and on many reserves you can get involved with helping) and diverse experiences and landscapes to explore.

Start your search for a responsible operator in South Africa at www.fairtrade.travel/South-Africa.

7 ECUADOR

This small South American nation is leading the way in sustainable travel, with operators who are focused on preserving both the indigenous way of life and the ecologically significant worlds of the Galápagos Islands and the Amazon rainforest. Your kids can learn all about the importance of evolution and why our lifestyles need to be sustainable, take a socially responsible tourist train (the Tren Ecuador) and use bikes to get down the famous Ruta de las Cascadas.

Learn more about how Tren Ecuador works and supports the local communities on its route at www. trenecuador.com.

8 KHAO SOK NATIONAL PARK, THAILAND

In Khao Sok National Park, you can show your children a different side of Thailand while minimising your family's effect on this incredible environment. Use a local guide to introduce you to the fascinating flora and fauna and make your base at one of the locally owned, community-focused lodges. You can even overnight in a rustic raft house on Chiaw Lan Lake, which involves using no electricity for the duration of your stay.
Active families will love the eco-friendly rafting, cycling, swimming and hiking at the Anurak Lodge. See www.anuraklodge.com.

9 TASMANIA, AUSTRALIA

Tasmania is a magical place for families. From treetop walks to messing about in boats, and from frolicking on the sand to the family-friendly 'Discovery Ranger' activities available in the national parks, there's plenty to keep everyone happy; and the beauty of it is distances are small.

There's also a strong ethos of using locally sourced (and delicious!) produce and a long-term sustainable approach to wildlife conservation and wilderness protection.
Follow @tasmaniaparks on Twitter or Facebook to keep up to date with family-friendly activities.

↑ 10 DUDE RANCHES, USA

Visiting a dude ranch (a working cattle ranch where visitors are welcome) is super-fun for families: there's a different pace to life (think of a day orientated around the farm jobs, out in the fresh air) and everyone can try something new, whether its horse riding, line dancing or fishing. As they are working farms, it's not hard to find a dude ranch that is focused on self-sufficiency and sustainability, and many work carefully to support the local community.
The Dude Ranch Association (www.duderanch.org) has a useful blog post on ranches with sustainable credentials.
• By Imogen Hall

WHAT DOES IT MEAN TO TRAVEL WELL?

Travel gives us so much: adventure, delicious food, expanded horizons and lasting memories being just a few of its personal rewards. Perhaps less obvious is the effect our travels have on the places and people we visit. In Travel Well, we explore how well-planned, sustainable travel can be a force for good for all involved – good for the environment, for the local people, and for ourselves.

WHAT IS SUSTAINABLE TRAVEL?

The World Tourism Organisation defines sustainable tourism as that which 'takes full account of its current and future economic, social and environmental impacts, addressing the needs of visitors, the industry, the environment and host communities.'

In this chapter we discuss ways our travel choices can benefit the destinations we visit. We present unforgettable journeys and experiences that have a low environmental impact; we look at how to spend the tourist dollar for the benefit of local communities; and we suggest meaningful and immersive tours that also help preserve ancient lifestyles and cultures. Travelling well requires thought and planning, but it offers the priceless opportunity of experiencing the riches of our planet all the while helping to preserve them for future generations.

LONELY PLANET'S

TRAVEL WELL

Should we all be flying less? / Travelling on a carbon diet
Going local, for the locals / Taking action on the road
Lessons from indigenous cultures / Hiking for meditation

SHOULD WE ALL BE FLYING LESS?

The UN has marked 2020 as a key deadline for reducing the world's carbon emissions, and most environmentalists agree that, for travellers, flying is the biggest emission contributor on an individual level. But what's a globetrotter to do? Those concerned by the effects of air travel can start by getting wise to the issue and the options available.

In 2020, the countries that signed up to the Paris Agreement will submit their long-term CO2 reduction plans to the UN's Intergovernmental Panel on Climate Change (IPCC). The IPCC has warned that 2020 is the year carbon emissions must peak, with a reduction (crucially) to follow, to prevent a global temperature rise of more than 2°C, which would lead to a detrimental rise in sea levels and extreme climate events from droughts to cyclones. The next set of targets is even more ambitious: emissions now need to be cut in half by 2030 and reach net zero by 2050. With aeroplanes contributing so significantly to carbon dioxide levels, there's no better time to re-evaluate our personal flying habits and start approaching air travel more thoughtfully.

Far from meaning an end to travel, a commitment to flying less can open up new horizons. Train journeys, electric vehicles, windjammer cruises, cycle tours, buses and even hiking all offer incredible ways to get from A to B at a lower emission cost, and most of the time you'll have a fantastic view of your destination as you travel through it.

• By Nora Rawn

FLYING SMART

Dreaming of a long-haul destination but worried about the impact of flying? Making small changes and planet-conscious choices can reduce your carbon footprint when you do fly.

TRAVEL LIGHT

Extra weight on planes burns fuel faster. Reducing your luggage by 15kg could save between 100 and 200kg of CO2 emissions on a return flight from London to Tenerife. Tempted to upgrade to business class? Be aware that economy class has the least environmental cost as it carries more people for the same amount of fuel.

GO DIRECT AND STAY LONGER

Since take-off and landing burns the most fuel, flying point-to-point without stopovers is the best way to reduce your carbon emissions when flying. Staying longer and travelling overland once you've arrived in your destination is also friendlier on the planet than taking short internal flights.

CHOOSE YOUR PLANE WISELY

Non-profit Atmosfair (www.atmosfair.de/en) has an Airline Index that ranks carriers by their fuel efficiency. Even better, look at your itinerary to evaluate the actual plane you'll be flying in (newer models are usually better). Flight comparison site Skyscanner (www.skyscanner. com) highlights flights with lower emissions.

TRAVEL BY TRAIN

Trains can offer a carbon saving of up to 90% over a flight between the same destinations, and the views can't be beaten. Hop aboard!

TOKYO TO HOKKAIDO, JAPAN

Speed from Tokyo to remote, snowy Sapporo in Hokkaido in just eight hours by means of the Shinkansen, with one seamless transfer en route. The contrast may give you whiplash, but the ride itself will be smooth as silk. Plus, Japanese high-speed trains, powered by nuclear energy, are substantially cleaner than diesel-powered lines.

AMSTERDAM TO ROTTERDAM, THE NETHERLANDS

National Dutch rail company NS (Nederlandse Spoorwegen) is now fully powered by wind energy: one windmill running for an hour is enough to power 190km of a rail journey. Take advantage by riding the rails from canal-side Amsterdam to historic port Rotterdam.

TORONTO TO VANCOUVER, CANADA

VIA Rail runs this 2266km journey through the Canadian Rockies and plains, providing extraordinary views without a need to navigate directions or stop for petrol on the way. Aptly titled The Canadian, the four-day route rolls through some of Canada's most spectacular scenery.

ELECTRIC TRIPS

The infrastructure for electric vehicles (EVs) has improved enormously over the last few years, making glorious and energy-efficient overland routes possible the world over.

↑ NATIONAL TOURIST ROUTES, NORWAY

Tour Norway's impossibly scenic roads behind the wheel of an EV. The country was an early adopter, and EVs here are almost entirely run on renewable hydropower.

THE GARDEN ROUTE, SOUTH AFRICA

The eight-hour holiday route from Cape Town to Port Elizabeth offers surfing, canoeing, diving, horse riding and hiking, with charging stations all the way.

BOARD THE BUS

Train travel gets all the attention, while the humble bus is slow and steady. Roads wind up mountains and across dusty deserts: a stress-free way around traffic and navigation. Look out the window and take it all in.

GREAT OCEAN ROAD, AUSTRALIA

One of the world's best-known drives isn't only for private, petrol-guzzling vehicles. VLine buses ply the route from Warrnambool to Melbourne via Apollo Bay and Geelong. Though service isn't daily, it takes the same gorgeous curves as the most dashing roadster.

RIO DE JANEIRO, BRAZIL TO LIMA, PERU

Expreso Internacional Ormeño's 6300km journey extends from the Pacific to the Atlantic and takes multiple days. As the longest bus route in the world, this nifty way to pass over the Andes without getting airborne will earn you significant bragging rights.

GO SELF-POWERED

Trains and buses may be lower carbon than either flying or driving a non-electric car, but for true eco-warriors, biking, kayaking or hiking through nature are a zero-emissions win.

GREAT DIVIDE MOUNTAIN ROUTE, USA

Cycle enthusiasts can bike from New Mexico to Alberta, Canada, on this 4455km endurance challenge that passes through the Rocky Mountains. It's a ride for the ages (and the iron-calved).

→ VANCOUVER ISLAND CIRCUMNAVIGATION, CANADA

Keen kayakers can paddle around Vancouver Island, nature-watching each day and camping on shore each evening. While the record for a self-supported circumnavigation is 12 days, outfitters run shorter trips along 110km Johnstone Strait.

HAUTE ROUTE, SWITZERLAND

From Mont Blanc to the Matterhorn, this classic path through the Pennine Alps is the best of all worlds: a walking route that takes in grand peaks and lets you sleep in cosy inns each night.

© RON WATTS / DESIGN PICS / GETTY IMAGES

TRAVELLING ON A CARBON DIET

It's a challenge to travel anywhere without leaving a carbon footprint, but by adding more planet-healthy choices to your travel diet, you can help to keep yours to an absolute minimum.

Gone are the days when sipping lurid cocktails through novelty plastic straws and stuffing our suitcases with single-use bathroom amenities signified nailing the art of travel.

With the global travel industry estimated to be responsible for nearly a tenth of global carbon emissions, taking conscious steps to reduce our carbon output on the road has never been so important. This hasn't always been a simple task, but as a growing number of destinations, hotels and other travel providers commit to greening up their act, it's becoming easier for globetrotters to support carbon-cutting leaders. Keep in mind that not all green claims are legitimate, so be sure to check them out before taking them at face value.

SLEEP GREEN

Required to reduce its emissions by a whopping 66% by 2030 to meet its Paris Agreement target, the global hotel industry needs your help to get there.

No longer does a water-saving commitment notice in a hotel guestroom give the property 'green' status. Today, accommodation providers that take sustainability seriously will outline their eco credentials (such as LEED – Leadership in Energy and Environmental Design – status) on their website. When the property's environmental commitment is not clear, or perhaps it doesn't have a website, ask questions. Not all hotels can afford the legwork involved in securing eco-certification, but many make efforts to minimise their impact via initiatives such as sourcing food and other supplies locally, eliminating single-use plastics, promoting recycling, offering water bottle refills, conserving water and energy and providing locals with meaningful employment opportunities.

Treating hotel rooms as you would your own home can also help to minimise emissions, for example, turning off lights and appliances when you head out, resisting the convenience of

© OTENTIC, MAURITIUS

unsustainable in-room freebies and requesting your linens aren't unnecessarily laundered.

If you feel your accommodation could make improvements, don't be afraid to provide constructive feedback, ideally in person – they can't evolve if they aren't aware they need to.

GO PUBLIC

We might be waiting a while for a more carbon-light alternative to air travel, but there are plenty of ways we can keep our emissions down when we arrive in our destination.

Where you feel comfortable, embrace public transport – not only can it be a travel experience in itself, but many cities use pedal-powered or electric vehicles, which reduces your impact even further. Some regions are also serviced by eco-friendly taxi companies – such as London's Green Tomato Cars (www.greentomatocars. com), the city's first and largest hybrid car service, and New Zealand's Green Cabs (www. greencabs.co.nz), which contributes a portion of each fare to native-tree-planting projects. If you need to hire a car, consider choosing a more planet-friendly electric, hybrid or fuel-efficient vehicle. Avoid driving at peak times, and keep an an eye on traffic updates with apps like Waze to help steer clear of fuel-guzzling traffic jams.

Finally, walking and cycling tours aren't just great carbon-neutral alternatives to bus tours, but they also facilitate deeper engagement with your destination.

WATCH YOUR CARBON CALORIES

Discovering new cuisines is one of the great joys of travelling, but with a quarter of global emissions coming from food, it's important not to lose sight of the effect of our food choices when exploring new destinations through our taste buds.

The easiest way to cut carbon calories is to avoid climate-damaging foods wherever you go, namely beef and other animal products, particularly if you can't be sure of the origin. The HappyCow app will help you locate plant-based and vegan options in more than 180 countries. Whatever you dine on, try to ensure it's local, seasonal, sustainable and ideally organic, all of which reduce the food's carbon output. When this isn't clear on the menu or the label, do your research. Sustainable seafood guides for nearly 30 countries can be found on the World Wildlife Fund website (wwf.panda.org).

Keen to save a bit of money? With homemade sandwiches found to produce half the emissions of shop-bought versions, self-catering can curtail your carbon impact, too. Packing your own reusable cutlery and crockery can also help you avoid the carbon cost of relying on single-use utensils on the road.
• By Sarah Reid

TEN AMAZING CARBON-FRIENDLY SLEEPS

KOLARBYN ECOLODGE, SWEDEN

Learn how to forage for your meals while staying in a cosy mud-and-grass cabin in the Swedish woods. There are no showers, but it does have a floating sauna! www.wildsweden.com/kolarbyn-ecolodge

← OTENTIC, MAURITIUS

The nation's only glamping outfit eschews plastic and grows its own produce at its two idyllic locations. https://otentic.mu

BARDIA ECOLODGE, NEPAL

Bed down at this affordable lodge made from local materials after a day tracking tigers in a remote national park. www.bardiaecolodge.com

JAO LODGE, BOTSWANA

Be among the first to experience this newly revamped safari lodge from the sustainable-tourism-award-winning Wilderness Safaris Botswana collection. https://wilderness-safaris.com

FEYNAN ECOLODGE, JORDAN

Enjoy traditional Bedouin hospitality at this stunning off-the-grid eco-hotel pioneer in the rugged Dana Biosphere. https://ecohotels.me/feynan

NIHI SUMBA, INDONESIA

Running entirely on house-made biofuel, this luxe beachfront resort empowers locals to protect the environment. https://nihi.com

1 HOTEL BROOKLYN BRIDGE, USA

This conscious New York City option has egg timers in the showers, boxes for donating unwanted clothes and a monthly 'dark sky' night when candles replace lights. www.1hotels.com

MASHPI LODGE, ECUADOR

Hang out with scientists at this beacon of sustainability in the Ecuadorian Choco. www.mashpilodge.com

← SWELL LODGE, AUSTRALIA

Run by wildlife photographers, this new Christmas Island eco-glamping retreat is the perfect base for experiencing the island's famous red crab migration. https://swelllodge.com

SLEEP GREEN, SPAIN

Reduce the tourism pressure on Barcelona by choosing this hostel committed to helping travellers reduce their footprint. http://sleepgreenbarcelona.com

GOING LOCAL, FOR THE LOCALS

Travelling in a responsible way doesn't need to be difficult; simply being careful about where you spend your money makes all the difference in the world. Choosing accommodation, guides, tours and souvenirs that are sustainable for the local community may require more research and forward planning, but you'll be helping your hosts while having a truly priceless travel experience for yourself.

Tourism accounts for about one in ten jobs globally and, according to the World Travel and Tourism Council, can disproportionately benefit those less well-off in society. With those powerful statistics in mind, there are many ways to ensure you make a positive contribution while immersing yourself in local culture and making incredible memories.

Opting for homestays over hotels puts money directly into the pocket of the community. And if you're concerned about overtourism, organisations such as fairbnb.coop (operating in Europe) will help ensure your holiday rental has a positive influence. If you need someone to show you around, choose a guide who lives in the area for unbeatable local expertise.

Being a sustainable traveller means staying away from the global restaurant chains and dining at independent venues you won't find anywhere else. It's one of the easiest ways to make a difference, and what could be more enjoyable than discovering a destination through your taste buds? It's also worth considering what you order from the menu. Often a destination's regional specialities use local ingredients instead of imported, meaning your money has double the positive effect (and you have a delicious meal). The same goes for drinks; independent craft breweries and wineries can turn a good meal into a great one. Try it all and you'll come home with plenty of local knowledge while leaving a meaningful legacy behind.

Carefully chosen souvenirs are a slice of culture you can take home with you. Best of all, buying something made in the area supports artists and craftspeople and can provide an economic incentive to continue plying a trade or craft at risk of dying out. Kutnu silk weaving from Turkey, ceramic art in Uzbekistan or colourful woven kunaa mats from the Maldives are just some examples of unique pieces you can treasure forever.

• By AnneMarie McCarthy

GUIDED BY LOCALS

With a little help from technology, it's never been easier to meet people. Get advice from the real experts by using these platforms to make connections with local residents.

↓ EAT WITH

Local hosts in over 130 countries will feed you in their own home (or sometimes rent a unique space). They'll often sit down to dine with you when the cooking is done, sharing their expertise. www.eatwith.com

TOURS BY LOCALS

This website connects tourists with friendly local guides worldwide. You can browse tour itineraries they've designed themselves or work with them to create your own bespoke one. www.toursbylocals.com

KEEPING CRAFTS ALIVE

Seeking out local artists and craftspeople for a unique memento will help sustain a community's creative industry, as well as sparking your memories for years to come.

JAM ART FACTORY, IRELAND

Everything in this Dublin gallery is created by independent artists, and their prints and homewares are guaranteed to bring a pop of colour to home in a budget-friendly way. www. jamartfactory.com

ABORIGINAL ART, AUSTRALIA

The Association of Northern, Kimberley and Arnhem Aboriginal Artists is a good place to start to discover Aboriginal art. It has more than 5000 members and 48 remote art centres it can connect you to. www.ankaaa.org.au

↓ MARY AND MARTHA, MONGOLIA

The team at this Ulaanbaatar organisation works long-term with local craftspeople to source a big selection of handmade and semi-handmade goods. They advise artists on all areas of the business as well as encouraging self-expression. www.mmmongolia.com

© RASTAFARI INDIGENOUS VILLAGE

COMMUNITY-BASED TOURISM

Immerse yourself in a different life by visiting small villages and towns, staying in homes and helping in community activities. You might come away with a whole new perspective on the world.

↑ RASTAFARI INDIGENOUS VILLAGE, JAMAICA

This vibrant community works with tour operators to welcome visitors for day trips. Expect to get involved in cooking, crafts, making music and learning about the importance of fire to the village. www.rastavillage.com

CHALALAN ECOLODGE, BOLIVIA

Visitors stay in the homes of villagers who then guide them around Madidi National Park. The locals now earn their money through tourism and safeguarding the environment instead of logging. http://chalalan.com

© MARY & MARTHA MONGOLIA

SUPPORTING PRODUCERS

Go straight to the source of the world's finest delicacies to put your money where your mouth is and have an unforgettable culinary experience. There are plenty of options for some delicious souvenirs too.

DENVER BEER TRAIL, USA

Denver is vying to be the ultimate American craft-beer destination, with more than 100 breweries, taprooms and brewpubs to explore. Time to consider going tank-to-table for your next meal.

RUTA DEL CAFE, PERU

Visit a number of coffee producers nestled in the stunning landscape of the remote Andes. You'll learn about the process from bean to cup, stay

on their family farms and, of course, buy directly from them. www.rutadelcafe.co

↓ DALMATIA'S WINE TRAIL, CROATIA

Croatia's light wines have a great reputation, thanks to the country's climate, but are never exported as domestic demand is too high. Most wineries are small with the owners on hand to meet and greet.

TAKING ACTION ON THE ROAD

For a socially switched-on generation in 2020, it's all about 'travel that matters'. By giving something back, we take a small but important step towards making the world an all-round better place, and a giant leap towards deeper cultural immersion and environmental awareness.

JOIN THE SOCIAL ENTERPRISE REVOLUTION

'You must be the change you wish to see in the world', said Gandhi. And if you've ever felt helpless when handing spare change to people sleeping rough on the streets, or worried over the plight of refugees, the good news is that you can play a part in changing the future of those who are disempowered or marginalised in society. In tune with the give-something-back zeitgeist, social enterprises are popping up at a rate of knots all over the world to give

less privileged people a more defined role in society and a brighter future. With a little pre-planning, you can easily track them down on your travels.

Many of these ethically minded projects are simple yet ingenious: guided tours run by the homeless lending a new perspective on a city, for instance, or coffee vans training them up as baristas. You can stay in boutique hotels staffed by refugees or disadvantaged women. Or choose to get your morning espresso in a cafe or lunch in a restaurant that employs asylum seekers. It's rewarding to know that whatever you spend is going some way to help someone get a new start in life.

LESS SELFIE, MORE SELFLESS

Some people shy away from the idea of volunteering, thinking they simply don't have time during their few precious weeks of holiday. Of course, if time isn't an issue, there are myriad ways in which you can help out, from wildlife conservation at a game reserve in Africa to construction volunteering in the wake of a natural disaster. But the truth is that there are thousands of bite-sized ways in which you can contribute when travelling, too: whether you have a few hours or days.

If you care about the coast, there are marine conservation beach clean-ups across the globe, where you can do your bit to tackle critically high plastic pollution levels simply by rolling up your sleeves for a morning.

Day volunteering schemes worldwide allow you to engage with local communities on a profound level, be it empowering women in Laos, helping out at a soup kitchen in Costa Rica, building homes in Bolivia, or upcycling

furniture in Mexico. Alternatively, there are schemes with a more environmental slant, ranging from sea turtle conservation in Costa Rica to caring for elephants in Thailand. So in just a day, it's possible to make a tangible difference, and it will most likely be the talking point of your entire trip.

BECOME A CITIZEN SCIENTIST

Scientific and environmental research needs enthusiastic volunteers now more than ever. Cue citizen science, a free and meaningful means of monitoring, measuring and recording everything from a rare species of wildlife to the night skies to assist scientists in gathering evidence-based data about the world in which we live, so as to better understand and protect it.

People-powered research is big and it's everywhere. If you're passionate about wildlife conservation, a quick search reveals scores of rewarding BioBlitz events, where you can join scientists and naturalists to find and identify as many species as possible in a designated area over a short period (usually 24 hours). This can be as intrepid as a rainforest expedition in the Amazon, or as easy as sharing and mapping bird sightings on your travels. Or if you fancy a little armchair travel, what could be more inspiring than helping to tag penguins and chicks in the Southern Ocean online?

Beyond this, there are small but significant initiatives, from stargazing to measure the brightness in the night sky to document light pollution to monitoring rainfall measurements in Nepal with a smartphone.

• By Kerry Walker

TEN WAYS TO TAKE ACTION ON YOUR TRAVELS

© EMMA'S TORCH

← EMMA'S TORCH, NEW YORK

Ethiopia, Haiti, Morocco – the dishes are as varied as the refugees that create them at this Brooklyn restaurant, empowering through culinary training. https://emmastorch.org

BEACHWATCH

The Marine Conservation Society's national beach cleaning program aims to turn the tide on litter in the UK. www.mcsuk.org/beachwatch

PENGUIN WATCH

Who doesn't love cooing over penguins and their chicks? Here's your chance to tag them online (among many other projects) and do your bit for conservation. www.zooniverse.org

GLOBE AT NIGHT

One for stargazers, this citizen-science project raises awareness of the effect of light pollution by inviting volunteers to measure night-sky brightness. www.globeatnight.org

→ INATURALIST

Get this handy app to collect photos, share your observations on nature and discuss your findings, perhaps as part of a BioBlitz event. www.inaturalist.org

SHADES TOURS, VIENNA

Get the inside scoop on Vienna's backstreets with eye-opening city tours led by homeless guides. www.shades-tours.com

FOUR BRAVE WOMEN, SYDNEY

This Summer Hill restaurant with a social cause helps refugee families to fund their own business through eight-week stints in the kitchen. www. thetradingcircle.com.au

LADYS FIRST, ZÜRICH

This boutique hotel near Lake Zürich empowers and employs disadvantaged women to give them a new start. www.ladysfirst.ch

EBIRD

Join the global effort to map bird ranges by sharing and logging sightings, photos and recordings on your travels. http://ebird.org

CHANGE PLEASE, LONDON

Swap the chain cafe for a more meaningful cup of joe at these coffee carts run by homeless people training to be baristas at different locations across London. www.changeplease.org

TRAVEL
WELL

BEST IN
TRAVEL
2020

LESSONS FROM INDIGENOUS CULTURES

Tours, homestays and educational experiences that are owned and run by indigenous peoples are on the rise, offering unforgettable opportunities to learn from and help preserve these ancient cultures. Is it time we all learned to sit down, ask the right questions, and listen to the wisdom of our elders?

On arrival in New Zealand, tourists are now asked to take the Tiaki Promise, pledging to be good stewards for the country's precious environment during their stay. *Tiaki* means 'to care for people and place' in the native language, te reo Māori. It's just one example of how the world's surviving first peoples have so much to teach the rest of us. First lesson for travellers everywhere: we were not bequeathed the Earth, we are mere custodians looking after it for the next generation.

Responsibly managed indigenous tourism – whether it be a bush tour, an arts centre, a homestay or an indigenous-led wildlife-watching trip – provides a platform for meeting the world's first peoples in a meaningful way, leaving you with a fascinating insight into and greater respect for the cultural heritage of your destination. In turn, your participation helps keep their arts, crafts and ancient lifestyle techniques alive for future generations.

When seeking indigenous tourism experiences, it's essential to do your research to ensure any experience is truly respectful, and that indigenous groups are actually involved and will benefit from any operation. In New Zealand, the national tourist board (www.newzealand.com) and Maori Tourism website (https://maoritourism.co.nz) both list a wealth of Maori-led tours. In Canada, the Aboriginal Tourism Association of Canada website (https://indigenouscanada.travel) lists three- to nine-day experiences, from village stays to arctic wildlife tours, all run by indigenous-owned businesses. In the vast state of Western Australia, the Western Australian Indigenous Tourism Operators Council (www.waitoc.com) is a great resource for Aboriginal tourism operators.

Perhaps the best reason for experiencing indigenous tourism is the opportunity to have your world view completely blown apart. Whether it's Australian Aboriginal astronomy, where the *dark* parts of the night sky make mythical stories, or Inuit survival skills deep in the Canadian arctic, or listening to the way people talk about time and place when their family has lived in a valley for millennia, not just decades...your perspective will shift when you ask the right questions.

• By Tasmin Waby

PERFORMING CULTURE

Music, dance and storytelling offer an exuberant introduction to indigenous culture.

GOROKO SHOW, PAPUA NEW GUINEA

Forget the Met Gala, the Goroko Show is the place to go for statement costumes, headdresses and original make-up designs. Only 60 years old, this annual show celebrates the traditions of 100 different tribes from across Papua New Guinea without the droll social-media commentary.

DJEMAA EL FNA, MOROCCO

Although overwhelmed by international visitors in peak season, the central square in Marrakesh – a Unesco 'Masterpiece of the Oral and Intangible Heritage of Humanity' – is the apotheosis of living culture, where storytellers, musicians and performers congregate daily in a chaotic live-action mash-up of traditional sounds and smells as they have for centuries.

TIEHUA MUSIC VILLAGE, TAIWAN

Taiwan has a rich indigenous heritage, with 16 traditional tribes sharing their culture, art and music. This uber-cool creative hub in the seaside city of Taitung hosts markets, exhibitions and live music performances, which keep the spirit of this place alive in an abandoned workers' dormitory, overlaying the new world with the old.

Aboriginal elder Willie Gordon gives tours of rock art around Queensland, Australia

HOMESTAYS

Stay under the same roof as your host for a window into local culture, all the while putting your tourist dollars straight into their hands.

GER TOURS, MONGOLIA

Experience the traditional pastoral lifestyle of the Mongolian steppes on a ger (yurt) tour. Saddle up your horse, help load a caravan of camel carts, and head across the Gobi grasslands to the next encampment.

NUNAVUT, CANADA

Want to know how the nomadic Inuit thrived for a thousand years in one of the most unforgiving climates on earth? It wasn't just through a nuanced understanding of snow and ice, but through innovation and collaboration, which is exactly what the Nunavummiut tourism industry in far north Canadian Quebec are doing today.

TOUNA KALINAGO HERITAGE VILLAGE, DOMINICA

Learn about the traditional food and medicines for good health from the Kalinago people on a homestay in the Touna Kalinago Heritage Village. Prearrange a herbal tour to receive their intricate knowledge of wild plants, meticulously observed.

→ MAJI MOTO MAASAI CULTURAL CAMP, KENYA

Experience the music, food and dance of the Masai Mara at this Maasai-owned and -operated camp. Your money will help fund local health, education and conservation efforts.

INDIGENOUS GUIDES

The insight imparted by knowledgeable guides into wildlife, landscapes and ancient legends forges deeper connections to a place.

RED CENTRE, AUSTRALIA

When visiting the Red Centre and Uluru, it's impossible not to leave in awe of Australia's first inhabitants and their spiritual relationship with the land and sky. In the desert at night, an Indigenous Astronomy tour will make you see the spectacular Milky Way with new eyes.

MADIDI JUNGLE LODGE, BOLIVIA

In Madidi National Park, brimming with wildlife, is a lodge created and sustained by
the indigenous Uchupiamonas community. Eco-tours such as birdwatching and night-time hikes bring this immense natural world to life through traditional knowledge and stories.

TAOS PUEBLO, USA

At Taos Pueblo in the Rio Grande valley of New Mexico you will find a living Native American community where visitors take guided tours of the original adobe settlements to learn about the rich history of this National Historic Landmark and Unesco World Heritage Site.

HIKING FOR MEDITATION

No mode of travel is more natural than walking; after all, we've been doing it ever since a distant ancestor in East Africa tried exploring the world on two legs instead of four. Fast forward a few million years and scientists are discovering there may be more to hiking than a pretty view.

WALK THIS WAY

Few activities can claim to heal the mind, body and soul. But in the search for an antidote to our stressful yet sedentary lives, the most ancient form of transport of them all has, as it were, a spring in its step.

Hiking is good for you. Very good – and in more ways than one. From Aristotle to Rousseau to Nietzsche, perambulating philosophers have often extolled the virtues of wandering (while wondering); now science is lending weight to their insights.

The physiological benefits of spending time outdoors are well documented; the related trend of shinrin-yoku or 'forest bathing', for example, is associated with lower levels of stress, lower blood pressure and a stronger immune system.

It doesn't take Socrates to see that hiking stiffens the sinews and summons up the blood, countering the slide towards a screen-focused existence. But did you know that this whole-body workout is also a boon for your brain?

NATURE CURES

Walking for prolonged periods of time can calm the chattering mind, and bring your focus back to the present; putting one foot in front of the other becomes a form of mantra, the equivalent of chanting 'om' repeatedly, except there is no agonising asana (yoga pose) involved.

A Stanford University study comparing people walking in urban environments to those walking in nature found that the latter experienced a decrease in their levels of anxiety and 'rumination', which is repetitive thought focused on negative emotions.

'This indicates that experiencing nature may have an impact on regulating emotion, which may help explain how it makes us feel better', according to the study's lead author, Gregory Bratman.

INNER CALM

William Mackesy, the creator of Walkopedia, an online resource for hikers, says sustained effort is the key to finding inner calm: 'You can achieve an interior quiet through a long trudge away from the busy world; special landscape helps but isn't essential. Or your mind can enter a contemplative zone when you hike through some resonant or numinous area – when on a pilgrimage trail, for instance.'

Hiking caters for all travel scenarios, too, whether you're in a group or going solo. Jennifer Pharr Davis, a former National Geographic Adventurer of the Year who has walked long-distance trails on six continents, said striding out alone was the first time she had ever experienced true peace of mind.

'There was no one around and no pressure to react, produce or respond. At first, it was awkward and unfamiliar, but the more I got used to it, the more I realised it was awesome.'

LEAVE ONLY FOOTPRINTS

It's a democratic activity as well. Buy a pair of boots and you're all set, wherever you live in the world, as there's likely to be a trailhead within striking distance. They're usually free to explore,

but even access to the planet's most popular hiking routes, where numbers are limited, costs comparatively little.

Furthermore, you can choose a challenge that suits your level, regardless of age or ability – from a flat stroll through the woods to an endurance-testing ascent of a mountain. Best of all, the only footprint involved in this experience is the one you leave behind in the mud; no carbon emissions, no travel-related guilt.

So perhaps it's time to put your best foot forward?

• By James Kay

TOP TEN FOR ZEN

← JORDAN TRAIL, JORDAN

A country-spanning, attraction-packed route from Umm Qais to the Red Sea, via the Dead Sea, Petra and Wadi Rum.

CAMINO FRANCÉS, SPAIN

This is the most popular version of the world's most famous pilgrimage route, running from the French Pyrenees to the heart of Galicia.

↙ WEST COAST TRAIL, CANADA

Ladders, boardwalks and staircases lead hikers past primeval forest, thundering waterfalls and storm-battered beaches on Vancouver Island.

MT KAILASH KORA, TIBET, CHINA

Erase a lifetime of sins on this short but challenging high-altitude circuit sacred to Buddhists, Hindus and Jains.

← THREE CAPES TRACK, AUSTRALIA

Hear the surf batter the base of vertigo-inducing cliffs on a tramp around the extremities of Tasmania's Tasman Peninsula.

VIA DINARICA, WESTERN BALKANS

A remarkable trek that unites old trails, shepherd's paths and military routes to cross the Dinaric Alps.

THE WESTWEG, GERMANY

Bathe in the enchanting and enchanted Black Forest on this north–south trail from Pforzheim to Basel.

JOHN MUIR TRAIL, USA

Follow in the footsteps of a true trailblazer on this sublime showcase of California's mountain scenery.

KUMANO KODŌ, JAPAN

Still your mind like a samurai on the sacred paths that wend and weave through the forests of the Kii Peninsula.

W TREK, CHILE

Patagonia's most celebrated route is a regional highlight reel of turquoise lakes, rolling pampas and spiky peaks.

INDEX

MAKING
BEST IN TRAVEL

Of all the amazing places and travel experiences on the planet, how do we choose the most exciting for the year ahead? It's a decision we do not take lightly. Read on for an overview of how the magic happens.

1 THE SURVEY

The annual Best in Travel survey is sent to the whole Lonely Planet family – every staff member, over 200 travel writers, bloggers, our publishing partners and more. In it we ask them to share their expertise on places and travel experiences that they predict will be buzzing in the year ahead.

2 THE TRAVEL HACK

We also organise brainstorming events in Lonely Planet offices the world over – from Běijīng to Buenos Aires. This is when we come together to discuss the subject that inspires us the most: travel. Where have we been? What are we excited about? Which destinations are

doing something special? Amid a flurry of Post-it notes and coffee cups, the Travel Hacks produce hundreds of ideas.

3 SHORTLISTING

The results of the survey and Travel Hacks produce a longlist of more than a thousand ideas. This is then reviewed by Lonely Planet's Best in Travel team – an opinionated bunch of travel geeks with hundreds of thousands of travel miles between them. The team read every pitch and help whittle down the list to a shortlist of the very best places.

4 THE PANEL

The shortlist is then sent to a panel of travel experts: five people who live and breathe

travel in their everyday lives.
They scrutinise each idea and
score them out of 100 for
topicality, excitement and
'wow' factor.

5 THE FINAL LIST

When the panel results are in,
the list is finalised and shared
with a trusted handful of people
at Lonely Planet until October
when, finally, the selection
of the best places and travel
experiences for the year ahead
is shared with the world.

Clockwise from left: brainstorming at
Travel Hack events in Seoul, Franklin,
Běijīng and Stuttgart

BEST IN TRAVEL 2020 JUDGING PANEL

. Mu Yun

Mu Yun was born in Běijīng. He has worked for Lonely Planet's China office since 2013 in many different roles, from author to translator, from commissioning editor to IT specialist. He has contributed to more than 60 Lonely Planet books, and occasionally writes for travel magazines. In his spare time, he is a contract travel photographer. With his wife and best travel mate, who is also an author for Lonely Planet, he travels around the world to explore historical sites and wildlife.

. Sarah Stocking

Before landing her dream job at Lonely Planet, Sarah spent many years travelling to the farthest places she could think of in search of the greatest adventures. From kayaking with humpbacks in Antarctica to making her own costume out of a banana tree to dance in the Tapati Rapa Nui on Easter Island, she never says 'no' to a new experience. In addition to her work as a digital editor in Lonely Planet's Tennessee office, Sarah has become Lonely Planet's resident family travel expert and loves the challenge of coming up with fantastic trips for her own family and others to enjoy.

. Kia Abdullah

Kia Abdullah is an author and travel writer based in London, UK. She has written two novels and contributed to *The Guardian*, *The New York Times*, BBC and Channel 4 News. Kia is a Lonely Planet Trailblazer and the founding editor of outdoor travel blog Atlas & Boots. She has visited more than 50 countries in pursuit of the world's best outdoor activities and believes nature is the best antidote to the stresses of modern life.

. Catherine Le Nevez

Catherine's wanderlust kicked in when she roadtripped across Europe from her Parisian base aged four, and she's been hitting the road at every opportunity since, travelling to some 60 countries and completing her Doctorate of Creative Arts in Writing, Masters in Professional Writing, and postgrad qualifications in Editing and Publishing along the way. Over the past decade-and-a-half she's written scores of Lonely Planet guides and articles covering Paris, France, Europe and far beyond. Her work has also appeared in numerous online and print publications.

. Martin Heng

Martin left England in 1987 and travelled for a decade before migrating to Australia to start a family. He has worked for Lonely Planet since 1999 in many different roles, including seven years as Editorial Manager, until a road accident in 2010 left him a quadriplegic. As Lonely Planet's Accessible Travel Manager he has published several accessible travel titles, including the world's largest collection of online resources for accessible travel. He has become a regular speaker at accessible travel conferences around the world.

ACKNOWLEDGEMENTS

PUBLISHED IN 2019 BY LONELY PLANET GLOBAL LIMITED

CRN 554153
www.lonelyplanet.com
978 1 78868 300 5
© Lonely Planet 2019
© Photographs as indicated 2019
Printed in Singapore
1 2 3 4 5 6 7 8 9 10

MANAGING DIRECTOR, PUBLISHING Piers Pickard
ASSOCIATE PUBLISHER Robin Barton
COMMISSIONING EDITOR Dora Ball
ART DIRECTION Daniel Di Paolo
LAYOUT DESIGNER Lauren Egan
EDITOR Bridget Blair
PROOFREADER Karyn Noble
IMAGE RESEARCHER Lauren Marchant
CARTOGRAPHY Michael Garrett, Wayne Murphy
PRINT PRODUCTION Nigel Longuet
COVER IMAGE © Filipe Frazao / Shutterstock
THANKS TO James Bainbridge, Joe Davis, Steve
Fallon, Tina García, Katie Johnson, Flora MacQueen,
Pablo Montes Iannini, Helena Rey De Assis, Jacob
Rhoades, Christina Webb

WRITTEN BY Joe Bindloss, Gregor Clark, Daniel James
Clarke, Laura Crawford, Alex Crevar, Belinda Dixon,
Peter Dragicevich, Megan Eaves, Bailey Freeman,
Joe Fullman, Sarah Gilbert, Chloe Gunning, Imogen
Hall, Tom Hall, Alexander Howard, Linda Ismaili, Mark
Johanson, James Kay, Jessica Lee, Stephen Lioy,
AnneMarie McCarthy, Carolyn McCarthy, Isabella
Noble, Matt Phillips, Nora Rawn, Sarah Reid, Andrea
Schulte-Peevers, Regis St Louis, Andy Symington,
Tasmin Waby, Kerry Walker, Clifton Wilkinson

STAY IN TOUCH lonelyplanet.com/contact

AUSTRALIA The Malt Store, Level 3, 551 Swanston
St, Carlton, Victoria 3053; 03 8379 8000

IRELAND Digital Depot, Roe Lane (off Thomas
St), Dublin 8, D08 TCV4

USA 124 Linden St, Oakland, CA 94607
510 250 6400

UK 240 Blackfriars Rd, London SE1 8NW
020 3771 5100

MIX
Paper from
responsible sources
FSC™ C021741

Paper in this book is certified against the
Forest Stewardship Council™ standards.
FSC™ promotes environmentally responsible,
socially beneficial and economically viable
management of the world's forests.

MAKE IT HAPPEN

Plan your 2020 travel with Lonely Planet

Switzerland

Argentina

Caribbean Islands

Morocco

Eastern Europe

West Africa

England

The Netherlands

Bhutan

Costa Rica

Ready to go after reading this year's Best in Travel list?
We've got a guidebook covering each of the top 10 destinations.